A practical guide to having children with Autism and Asperger's Syndrome

By Sarah Sprules

This book is dedicated to my amazing children who continue to astound me and make me laugh every day. For my husband, my family and my chosen family, my best-friend Sarah for their continued love, belief and support.

It is also of course, dedicated to the children on the spectrum and their warrior parent/carers who fight a daily battle that most never see or appreciate.

Contents

Introduction

If your child has been given a diagnosis of being on the autistic spectrum it can be a little overwhelming to say the least, even if it was what you were expecting. One parent said to me that it was like getting on a plane and ending up in a different country than the one you expected, and you don't know how to speak the language. Another said to me that you have to take time to grieve for the loss of the child you thought you were going to have. Every parent/carer deals with the diagnosis in their own way. In the beginning, you have so many questions and you could easily spend a fortune buying recommended text books full of academic jargon; which can seem like a never-ending labyrinth of information and opinions and that's even before all of the web surfing.

This was how I felt when my son was diagnosed with Asperger's Syndrome (AS) at the age of five. I was trying to navigate him through having AS and being in a mainstream school and I had no idea how I was supposed to represent him against trained professionals when I didn't know anything about autism. All I knew was my son, not a diagnosis or a set of traits. One head teacher said to me that she didn't know how I coped with my son at home which left me speechless, what else was I supposed to do, he was my son.

I attended various courses and I know was lucky to have the opportunity, there are hugely long waiting lists to get help and my friends who lived in other areas, had no access to help at all simply because of the council boundary they lived in.

Three years later my daughter was also diagnosed as an Aspie. The children were receiving some help at school, but I started to wonder where was the help for the parent/carers? Where were our interventions?

Over the last eight years I have been on a journey of autism education and discovery, which included working as one to one support for children with autism in mainstream schools, as I wanted there to be at least one person in the school who truly understood what they were going through. I have written books about autism and now I am currently studying for a BSc in Child and Adolescent Mental Health and I have a passion to help other parent/carers, especially those who have no idea where to turn to and need help.

Following many coffee mornings listening to parent/carers who were exhausted and didn't know where to turn, I decided that it was time to draw together all of the knowledge I've gained and write a book which would help empower parent/carers to support their children. I wanted to give them some answers or at least signpost them to where they could find out more about the practical considerations of being an autism parent/carer.

I wanted this book to be easy to read, non-patronising, informative, light-hearted and part memoire from someone who understood, rather than a stale academic book that is hard to read and even more difficult to identify with. Each child is different, autism is a vast spectrum and I hope I have covered as much as possible that will be of use to you.

So, from me to you I hope this helps you in your own personal journey into the spectrum. It's going to be one heck of a ride.

Autism, Asperger's Syndrome and High Functioning, what does it all mean?

Over the years there have been different terms used to diagnose autism. Recently there has been a move away from the term Autistic Spectrum Disorder (ASD) as the word 'disorder' has been deemed offensive. Similarly, Asperger's Syndrome is less used as a term although some professionals still continue to use it.

The new definitions are Autism 1, 2 and 3. Autism 1 is for high functioning and those who would previously have been diagnosed with Asperger's Syndrome and is characteristic of having more advanced language skills. Autism 2 is for those requiring more support than someone at Level 1, have very narrow interests and low language skills. Autism 3 is the equivalent of the previous Autism Spectrum Disorder diagnosis and covers those who need more support than the other classifications and are non-verbal or have extremely limited language and get very distressed when faced with change or transitions. Whichever diagnosis term has been used for your child, there are similar core symptoms, and all come under the autism umbrella.

Autism is a disability that a person is born with, although symptoms may not be seen until later in a child or even an adult's development. When my son was diagnosed I looked into the causes of autism and as with so many of my questions, I found a lot of opinions but no definitive answer. Whenever I spoke to professionals, I was asked questions such as "did you have a natural birth?" or "did you bond with your child?" This line of questioning initially led me to see my son's diagnosis as being affected in some way by me and I was upset by this. When I started connecting the dots however, I came to the eventual conclusion, that in our case there was a definite genetic link. At the time I even thought it was possibly the result of my son having just been given his regular childhood immunisations.

When my daughter was born, I delayed her MMR immunisations and when she was about eighteen months or, so it was obvious that she too had Asperger's Syndrome. She was formally diagnosed by the age of three and her MMR followed promptly after. Although it may seem irresponsible to have left her unvaccinated in her early years, I'm glad that it happened that way, as I knew for sure that it wasn't a result of the MMR vaccine that she had Asperger's. It just so happens that the signs emerged around the same age as my children were being immunised.

Of course, it is possible to help a child to learn to cope better and manage their autism more effectively, but contrary to the question that I have been asked several times, no there is no cure. It is a lifelong condition and no my children are not going to grow out of their Asperger's.

Autism is characterised by a lack of social communication, rigidity of thought and difficulties with social interactions. Children with ASD normally have delayed speech, learning difficulties, lack of motor skills and are less likely to make eye contact. Those with AS do not have language difficulties and their symptoms although similar to those with ASD, are generally less severe.

Professionals you might meet

If your child is being assessed for autism or has just received a diagnosis then you will most likely come into contact with professionals that you've probably never encountered before and sometimes parent/carers can feel a little overwhelmed or even ambushed when they walk into a meeting and are suddenly confronted by an assured person with an official title and although you might not know exactly what it is they do, they seem to have an opinion on your child and what is best for them. It may help to be aware of the terms used and a brief overview of what they mean.

Educational Psychologist – An Educational Psychologist commonly referred to as an Ed Psych will be called in by the school to help a child who has been identified as potentially having a special need and may require a diagnosis. The Ed Psych will spend time observing the child and will assess whether the child needs further referral. They work with other agencies when necessary, such as social workers to create support and possibly interventions for the child. An Ed Psych report may be required for a diagnosis, or for schools in particular to access additional help for the child by way of an Educational Health and Care Plan (EHCP) which is required if your child is to attend a specialist school. There are often long waiting lists for an appointment with an Ed Psych.

Speech and Language Therapist – A Speech and Language Therapist also known as an SLT does not only deal with speech and language difficulties, they also help children who have issues centred around eating and drinking. SLTs also often contribute to autism assessments. Due to austerity cuts SLT teams are under pressure through lack of funding and rising need, which in some areas can lead to children not meeting the threshold of requirements as they are so high. Those that do meet the thresholds and are able to be seen, may only receive an initial assessment from a qualified SLT before some goals are handed to the child's teaching assistant to practice with them until the SLT returns several weeks later to assess their progress. In my experience of working in schools as a teaching assistant, finding the time to carry out regular speech and language therapy isn't easy, and the child is often put at a disadvantage as the teaching assistant almost certainly doesn't have the necessary skills which are required to provide Speech and Language support. Speech and Language therapy can be very beneficial for those children who are lucky enough to work with a qualified therapist.

SENDCo – Every school is required to employ a Special Education Needs Co-ordinator referred to as a SENCo. Increasingly they are also known as a SENDCo with the D standing for disabilities or in some cases Inclusion Co-ordinators. The role of the SENDCo is to oversee Special Educational Needs (SEN) and to ensure that the school are adhering to SEN policy. A SENDCo must be a qualified teacher, who has undertaken further SEN training. The SENDCo acts as a go-between for the school and the parent/carers. They will also liaise with other agencies if there are any involved with the child, such as Autism Outreach; which are autism specialists that schools can contact for additional support. It can be difficult to speak to a head teacher so if you have concerns and are unable to speak to the class teacher, the SENDCo will be a good person to make an appointment with. They possess a great deal of SEN knowledge and can be on hand if there is a problem during the school day and can be a consistent point of contact.

Community Paediatrician – Community Paediatricians are experts in development and disabilities in children and behavioural issues, they can be vital in diagnosing a child with autism. Waiting lists to see a Paediatrician can run into the hundreds and it can be difficult to obtain an appointment.

Occupational Therapist – An Occupational Therapist (OT) helps a child with their motor skills, such as handwriting, which children on the spectrum can find difficult. Schools usually arrange for OTs to visit the child at school if they require support.

CAMHS – In some areas, Child and Adolescent Mental Health Services or CAMHS as they're commonly known are responsible for diagnosing autism. However, you may only be in contact with CAMHS if your child has difficulties which affect their mental health, such as anxiety. As with other professionals CAMHS are heavily oversubscribed and have extremely high thresholds and waiting lists.

Getting a diagnosis

Different local authorities have their own particular processes for getting a diagnosis which can vary greatly. In fact, both of my children experienced different diagnostic routes in the same local authority, simply because they were diagnosed three years apart.

My son was diagnosed in two thousand and ten, following two years of being assessed by a Community Paediatrician as a consequence of a referral by our GP and various school visits by the Ed Psych and a SLT. The two years spent following the assessment process was a particularly stressful time, which wasn't helped by the fact that we didn't always see the same person, as our Paediatrician only worked part time.

With my daughter it was completely different, even though she was assessed in the exact same building as my son had been diagnosed three years previously. At the time, our local council was trialling an Autism Spectrum Assessment Team (ASAT). I spent an hour in a room with a Paediatrician and a SLT who assessed my daughter using an Autism Diagnostic Observation Schedule (ADOS) whilst interviewing myself in the same room and at the end of the hour, she was given a diagnosis of Asperger's Syndrome and Pathological Demand Avoidance.

I was told over and over again by professionals that labels didn't help and there was no need to try to get one, I didn't agree with that opinion. How can you deal with something? Research something? How do you help others understand? If you don't know what it is that you're dealing with in the first place? Personally, I would have felt like a fraud if I had invited myself along to support groups and sat talking to parent/carers who actually did have diagnosed children. I felt it would have looked like we were just attention seeking. Getting a diagnosis was the key that unlocked the support and empathy my children needed. My local NHS team runs an autism course for parents of newly diagnosed children which was a great source of empowerment. Unfortunately, they have a huge waiting list and sessions run for three months and are only held during weekday mornings which are inaccessible for working parent/carers.

For my family, getting a diagnosis came as a huge relief. We finally had a name for why our children were different to their peers, which was even more important for them than it was for us. It's amazing the level of understanding we received once we mentioned the 'A' word to people. There is still a long way to go, but there is far more autism awareness in society's consciousness than at any time before. Personally, I think this has a lot to do with the number of celebrities who have raised the profile of autism and the sheer number of children being diagnosed.

One of the things that parent/carers agonise over, is the if or when to tell the child about their diagnosis. I have been a part of many discussions concerning this and the general consensus seems to be that there is no right or wrong answer. Each decision needs to be made on an individual basis and the main reason for this is the child's cognitive ability to understand the diagnosis.

Some parents judge that their child is happy as they are, and they do not want to explain to the child that they have a disability. For some parent/carers it can be a struggle to accept their child's diagnosis and they are simply not ready to have conversations about the subject. For us it was pretty straight forward. Even before my son was formally diagnosed, we used the word autism around the house in reference to TV characters etc, I wanted him to think of it as an every-day word and not something that was taboo. At the time, his mainstream school disagreed with this decision.

When he was diagnosed, I left a leaflet on the table about autism and Asperger's and because he'd been able to read Harry Potter at the age of four, my son was curious about everything he read and wanted to know more about these two terms. I explained autism and Asperger's in terms he could understand at the age of five and he turned to me and said, "that's me, I'm a Battenberg!" I laughed and corrected him, and he said the word Asperger's a couple of times and then started talking about something else.

Over the following days, weeks, months and years we explained what being an Aspie meant for him and it empowered him to think of himself as part of a super-hero group of intelligent beings. He was also able to understand why he got angry or couldn't do certain things like his peers and this allowed him to not be so hard on himself. When my daughter was diagnosed we told her that she had Asperger's and she just shrugged and said that she was pleased, because it meant that she was like her brother.

Because of the high level of need and the low level of resources waiting lists to be seen for assessment can be up to two years in some areas. Nobody gives birth to a baby and hopes it is going to be diagnosed with a disability and it angers me to hear ignorant people talking about autism diagnoses as though you can just get one out of a cereal box. If your child's behaviour or mental health is deteriorating, then keep calling whichever professional is responsible for assessing your child. That old saying is definitely true in this case, it's the squeaky wheel that gets oiled first. Don't sit there passively waiting your turn if things are getting worse.

For the remainder of this book, the word autism will include those with ASD, AS, High Functioning Autism and Autism 1,2,3; unless otherwise stated and the word parent will include parents and carers.

Understanding the symptoms

You might hear the term 'triad of impairments' used quite a lot when discussing autism. The triad are the three symptoms all need to be experienced in order to gain a diagnosis. The impairments are Social Interaction, Social Communication and Social Imagination/Flexibility of Thought. In other words, if your child has problems talking or interacting with others; if they cannot hold a conversation without appearing 'rude' or 'aggressive' etc and they have very rigid thought processes such as only wanting to talk about Sonic the Hedgehog for example, then these could be the indicators of them being somewhere on the spectrum.

People with autism experience and process the world in a different way. For instance, one little boy I worked with referred to pain in colours. He frequently got throat infections and he would start the day by telling me what colour his throat was. If it was red or purple, I knew he was in pain. Although it is classed as a disability, children with autism can be amazing, inciteful, inspiring and astounding. They are different to others, not less than others.

The science of it all

Autism research is continuing to grow, as never before and strives to improve the lives of those on the autistic spectrum. Current research indicates that it is possible to accurately predict autism from the age of three months, which has huge implications for diagnosing children. As awareness and training has improved, the number of children being diagnosed with autism is rapidly increasing. Better awareness of the symptoms of autism is one reason for the increase in diagnoses, but many also believe it is the difficulties of the modern 'social media' world we live in which is causing the dramatic rise in numbers.

The investment into current research is prompting a move away from considering the causes of autism and is instead focusing on how to improve services for the daily lives of those with autism.

I often say to my son that he is overthinking something that really should be simple. He did a search online and found two MRI scan pictures and showed me the difference in someone with Asperger's and someone with no neurological differences and the comparison was amazing. The scan of someone was without special needs, i.e. typically developing (TD) showed a small area of colour, but the Aspie's scan was lit up like a Christmas tree. My son just left the pictures on my desk as a subtle reminder not to tell him he overthinks everything, he can't help it. This can be a double-edged sword, the ability to overthink can be invaluable for problem-solving, yet it could also cause anxiety and sleep problems.

What you might come across

A list of autistic traits would fill more space than this book has space for, however I thought it would be helpful to list the most common. If you see your child exhibiting some of these traits you will be able to recognise it as part of their autism and hopefully feel a little more in control because you understand what is causing the behaviours.

Waking up angry – It always amazed me that my children could actually wake up angry. When I envisaged having children I always imagined these little people bouncing out of bed and eating their cereal around a table, all perfectly dressed in their school uniforms excited to go out and greet the day, whilst I drank orange juice and cartoon animated bluebirds helped me with the housework.

   In reality, I would tiptoe in to my son's room, gently kiss the top of his head and then get my head bit off by this snarling angry child and things would deteriorate from there. Children with autism suffer with sleep problems far more than their TD peers and so they are less likely to wake up feeling refreshed. Also, from their perspective, mornings are one of the most chaotic and stressful parts of the day with lots of expectation and time constraints placed on them. They get rudely awoken and then feel annoyed at you for waking them up. If it is a school day then they are most likely to have demands hurriedly fired at them. Understandably the child is going to be even more annoyed by you chivvying them along when it is a school day. Often, time can be an abstract notion to children on the spectrum and they won't wish to be hurried, especially when the end result is that they have to go to school. Adding into the anger and frustration is the fact that the demands put upon them are things that are generally uncomfortable. Minty toothpaste can often make them feel sick, especially when mixed with breakfast too soon before or after. The actual act of brushing their teeth can physically cause pain. Children on the spectrum also often have a fear or water or dislike showering or bathing, which can also cause distress.

   Whilst their TD peers are generally more independent, children with autism can struggle with motor skills which can make getting dressed something of a struggle. Another problem can be caused by hypersensitivity in feeling, which can make wearing socks or tops and trousers with scratchy labels and seams almost impossible. Making choices such as what to have for breakfast can also be overwhelming. When you consider all of these things, it's no wonder that our children can find mornings difficult and although there may be a time limit to work to, understanding and patience can make the start of the day a little easier. Visual timetables can also help, so that the child knows what is expected and can follow the routine without having to remember what to do and in what order.

Problems with turn taking – Taking turns in conversations, playing games that require social interaction, social communication or patience and understanding of other people's needs and wants are all things that children on the spectrum are more likely to struggle with. Winning and losing are also very difficult. If they win it can cause them to gloat and seem almost arrogant to their peers and if they lose this can be almost impossible to cope with for some children. Their response to losing can be disproportionate, such as meltdowns, tantrums, tears and aggressive behaviour. I've lost count of the number of times that our Monopoly board has gone flying across a room, or a game console controller gets rammed into the floor in anger. My son understands that we don't have a bottomless pit of money and that we might not be able to immediately replace anything that he has broken, but when he loses a game his face turns red, tears stream from his eyes and he is completely unable to control himself. Even if game time normally results in flying game pieces or controllers it is still worth persevering, as this is a skill that will aid them in the future and is easier to deal with when they are still relatively small. Keeping calm and using a soothing voice to try and diffuse the situation and letting them win at least half of the time where possible should help to begin with. It may also be something that the school can help them to work on.

Control – Children don't have a lot of control over their own lives, they are dependent on adults for when they eat and drink and at school even have to get permission to use the toilet. However, they are quick to understand how to gain what power they can for themselves. This isn't exclusive to children with autism, but symptoms are more severe in children on the spectrum, especially those with Pathological Demand Avoidance (PDA).

The areas where children can generally always get the attention of an adult is by acting out and misbehaving, toileting and feeding. If a child is not acting appropriately then an adult will soon focus in on them and the same can be said for when a child is eating and going to the toilet. If a young child says they want to go to the toilet, especially when they are toilet training the parents or nursery/school staff are guaranteed to come running and for several minutes that child has their undivided attention and can be the subject of a lot of praise and possible reward. Eating can have the same effect, parents in particular can get quite tense over how much their child has or hasn't eaten. It is best not to make mealtimes a battleground and to remain calm if possible. Sometimes children with autism can reject food because of it colour, texture or temperature. My son would not eat anything with sauces and could not eat pasta shapes unless they were perfectly formed, he also could not eat anything unless the temperature was just right and earned himself the nickname Baby Bear when he was little. We also had to get a little plate with divided sections so that his food wasn't touching, such as the beans not touching the chicken nuggets etc. It can be easier to send them to school with packed lunches, so you can ensure they're eating something they like and also, you are able to see exactly how much they've eaten at the end of the day. When my son was little we gave him a liquid multi vitamin as a supplement, as he ate such a restricted diet. As the child gets older, if eating is still a problem there is the risk the child might develop an eating disorder and a GP may need to be consulted.

Eating – Children with autism are prone to gastrointestinal problems and stomach aches can be common. They are also more likely to experience food allergies and have issues centred around eating. Some children will only eat food of a certain colour, or texture and have a very restricted diet. These issues can lead to an eating disorder, so be aware of whether they may need extra support and never force them into eating something they don't want.

When my son was young he only liked to eat pasta and pesto or kedgeree, yet if he ate them too often he would claim to be bored and refused to eat anything. Parents of TD children often say, 'they'll eat when they're hungry.' I wish this was the case for all children, but it's not. My son looked so undernourished and we were desperately trying to get him to eat, whilst giving him multivitamin supplements. He wouldn't eat anything that had a sauce and refused all temptations to vary his diet. Much to my amazement, he began to eat different foods, but only if his favourite characters ate them. One night he asked me for a grilled cheese sandwich because Greg from Diary of a Wimpy Kid ate them. He happily ate chilli hotdogs because Sonic the Hedgehog ate them and after watching Heston Blumenthal he was inspired to eat curry.

If your child has issues with food, keep trying to tempt them into eating different things, as they mature they might get braver.

Meltdowns – I've talked about meltdowns to parents of TD children and some of them have said "oh yeah my son used to have tantrums too." For anyone who has witnessed a genuine meltdown, they would know it is NOTHING like a tantrum. Even for a parent, a meltdown can be intimidating to deal with. A meltdown happens when a child is so distraught and overwhelmed that they cannot use rational thought processes and are completely out of their own control. Meltdowns are not a conscious choice and are a loss of reasoning capability and children should never be punished for having a meltdown, although they may need time to calm down by themselves afterwards.

If possible, it may be a good idea to reflect on what happened to trigger the meltdown and talk it through with your child if appropriate. Don't attempt to talk to them until a good while after the meltdown has finished, it takes a lot longer for the child's emotions to become regulated and calm once more and you don't want to remind them too soon of what made them so anxious in the first place.

Impulsivity – Children on the spectrum can be very impulsive. Whether this is rushing around from the slide to the swings in a playground, or to changing jobs or even partners as they get older it is characteristic of autism and they will need help in managing this. I was called into my son's nursery once to be told by his Key Worker said that his impulsiveness frightened the other children. Role modelling can be a good way of helping a child to manage their impulsivity. When they exhibit a good behaviour, then a token or reward may help as motivation. Children can be more impulsive when they are overwhelmed, so distracting them with something calming can help reduce impulsive behaviours.

Mind blindness – Also known as Theory of Mind. Mind blindness is something that people on the autistic spectrum are commonly affected by. It is the inability to understand that other people have their own thoughts and feelings. This is a cause of anxiety and a barrier to communication if the child is unable to predict someone else's movements, behaviour or emotion. Socially, Theory of Mind causes difficulties if a person you are trying to interact with does not consider you and can appear abrupt or rude and this can cause conflict with peers. Through talking about other people's emotions, relevant books and roleplaying, you can help your child to develop better Theory of Mind skills.

Running – Children with autism are more likely to be completely oblivious to hazards and danger. For some, there is no alarm bell that something might cause them harm. They can be so focused on going from A to B and if there is a road in the middle, they may just walk out without realising.

Another issue can be running away, not only do they not appreciate the hazards they can even think of this as a fun game. I've been in the supermarket and my two-year-old daughter thought it would be fun to initiate a game of chase and I had to choose between my handbag and trolley full of shopping whilst my beloved daredevil who's faster than me was squealing in delight. For years, I did my shopping online, so I could avoid this from happening again.

Bribery sometimes works wonders and your child might be persuaded to listen to you if they might get a small treat. Other children might not be able to understand the expectation and more physical restraints such as wrist reins or little backpacks with reins attached can be cheaply bought online and may help.

Running away may be an even more serious problem if the child is running away from school or home. Some schools have signs up on the door reminding the child not to leave the room by themselves or have locked gates to prevent a child leaving the grounds. When my son was younger we used to leave the chain on the front door when we were at home to prevent him from leaving, after a particular incident. We lived two doors away from a sweetshop and one morning I popped my coffee cup into the kitchen and came back into the living room to find the front door wide open. My son was nowhere to be seen and after five seconds which felt like ten years I found him in the nearby shop with a huge smile on his face and so a chain was necessary.

Children with autism are very perceptive and it didn't take him long to realise he could move a chair to the door and take the chain off, so in the end we had to lock the door when we were inside and hang the keys on a nail very high up which wasn't ideal in terms of fire safety, but it was what we had to do at the time to protect our son.

Upset by change – Change can be very difficult for children with autism to deal with. We can't predict the future and there are certain things we can't control such as road closures yet when managed, children can be prepared for the changes and manage them much easier. Visual timetables are a good way of letting a child know what is going to happen and explanations and even dry runs of a journey as early as possible are best for positive outcomes. Schools are such busy places and there are so many children to consider but working with the school to ensure they notify your child of change is so important. I always say to people that there's nothing wrong with my children, it's other people's actions that cause the problem, so getting school on board will be vital. I lost count of the times that my son lost play-times because he reacted negatively when he wasn't warned about changes in advance.

Lack of Sleep – Children with autism suffer from sleeping disorders more than those without autism, this has definitely proved to be the case in our home. One reason that children with autism have sleep issues is that their bodies do not produce the hormone melatonin which helps our bodies to sleep. Melatonin rises in the body in response to darkness, and this process is thought to be disrupted due to the light from screens. My son is thirteen and my daughter is eight, but neither of them has slept through for a full night, despite keeping them in a routine and away from screens before bedtime, all of their lives.

As anyone who has had a baby knows, sleep deprivation is terrible and debilitating. It can prevent you from concentrating and thinking properly, it can cause irritability, but the knowledge that it won't last is a lifeline to hold onto. For those with autistic children you may have no idea when you'll ever get a full night of sleep ever again. I'm starting to think that my daughter will still be lying next to me sleeping with her arms and legs spread out like a star fish when she's nineteen.

Even as young babies, my two never took naps during the day like other children. Good natured friends and relatives made comments such as "he'll sleep well tonight", when they've seen my son running around all day constantly on the go and in the beginning, I naively hoped they'd be right. Unfortunately, whenever my children were full of energy during the day, it always made them even more wide awake in the evening and they'd desperately need to sleep but were so overexcited they couldn't sleep.

I quickly got annoyed by others who appeared to subtly blame me for the lack of sleep my children got. Those without autistic children thought it was simply a case of getting them into a routine, if only it were that simple. I would take the children up at eight o'clock in the evening, after having given them a bath and bedtime story and lay in the dark without any stimulation and yet they would still be wide awake eleven o'clock at night and then wide awake again at half five in the morning, despite waking several times in the night. After a few years I tried a different approach and took them up at a later time, so that they would be more exhausted and fall asleep quicker. This unfortunately didn't go as planned and they were awake until midnight.

Another common problem that we also have is getting our children to stay asleep throughout the night. My daughter casually strolls into our room every day at one or two in the morning and claims she's bored. Melatonin can be prescribed by a GP, but like any medication there are side effects and so any decision should be carefully considered. Some children are simply so stressed just getting through the day that they are exhausted and so they oversleep. There are many different types of sleep disorder, so if your child is having problems getting to sleep or staying asleep, then speak to a professional such as a Health Visitor, GP, Paediatrician, SENDCo.

Sleep problems are probably not going to be fixed overnight, but here's some tips to try before approaching a professional. A visual timetable of the day, which shows when it is bed time can be a good place to start in trying to let a child know that there is a time for sleep. You could add in putting on pyjamas, cleaning teeth and having a bath, so that it teaches the child to get into a routine. A sticker or reward chart may also help for motivation. Start helping them to wind down prior to bedtime, by encouraging quiet activities such as reading to keep them as calm as possible. Stop them from watching screens for two hours before bed, which I know is easier said than done. Avoid caffeine before bed as children on the spectrum can be more susceptible to the effects than their TD peers and caffeine can remain in the system for up to eight hours. Try to reduce drinks just before bedtime so that they are not awoken in the night by the need to use the toilet. In the summer, blackout curtains can be useful in blocking out light, especially first thing in the morning.

Haircutting – Having a haircut for a child with autism can be extremely stressful (and for their parents). I tried to get my son into a haircutting routine from about six months onwards as he was born with a full head of hair. I even found a hairdressing salon where the children sat in chairs that looked like a 3D racing car placed in front of screens so that he could watch a DVD to distract him.

Unfortunately, it still didn't help. He still screamed the place down every time anyone with a pair of scissors came near him. For those with hyper-sensitivity, cutting hair can cause physical pain and can be very traumatic.

My hairdresser told me recently that she cuts the hair of several teenagers with autism. She explained how she cuts their hair in their bedrooms whilst they play on their games console, because otherwise their parents stand no chance of getting them into a salon.

Patience, understanding and reassurance are key and finding the right hairdresser or barber is essential. Some children may experience anxiety at the unknown, or because someone is putting blades in close proximity to vulnerable parts of them, such as their ears or their eyes. If they sit calmly and then suddenly move their head and get caught by the scissors or a razor it could prove their worst fears and they won't trust anyone to cut their hair again. Another problem is that if they go to a barber they have to sit and wait for an undefined amount of time, which can be impossible for some children. Once you've found the right person to cut your child's hair, then it would be a good idea to either visit the salon or shop or even let them visit you if they are going to be cutting the hair in your home and simply spend time talking through what will happen at the actual appointment. Knowing what they're going to use to cut the hair, what product might be used and why and what will happen and when, can go a long way to easing anxiety and making the appointment less traumatic for all.

Sitting still – Children on the spectrum can find it very difficult to sit still, especially for extended periods of time. We couldn't go out to a restaurant for a meal when my children were little, unless they had portable games consoles and then they would sit quietly and still just long enough to wait for the food to be cooked. Eventually, we found all you can eat restaurants which are amazing if you have restless children. People are up and down out of their seats all of the time, so no one even notices that your child is moving around. In fact, we found that our son actually ate more because he felt relaxed and was ready to try different things.

Sitting on the carpet or in assembly at school can be a flashpoint for children. Often, they are bored, distracted and fidgety and get noticed by a member of staff and told to sit still. Shouting at a child with autism to sit still is not helpful or effective. Wiggle seats can be purchased on line and can provide a child with a base that makes them feel comfortable and can help them sit still and focus for longer.

Impact on siblings – It has been suggested that divorce rates are higher in families of children with a disability and are highest for families where at least one child has autism. This is one trend that I hope to not follow. There is a lot of awareness surrounding the effect on parents, but they are not the only ones impacted by autism in the family, often the effect on siblings is unintentionally overlooked. It can be difficult for some families to manage a child's behaviour, especially if that child doesn't sleep well or challenges every decision or request. It is mentally and physically exhausting and often there is little time or energy left over for anything or anyone else. The need for the child with autism to control can either cause their sibling to feel dominated, or cause friction and arguments as both vie for control.

The sibling may feel resentful at the amount of time and attention that is given to their sibling with autism. Explaining that the child with autism may need a little more help, but that it isn't their fault can be difficult if the sibling is too young to understand. However, it's still an important message and one worth repeating. As the sibling grows older, they will hopefully learn to understand and not feel so resentful of their brother or sister.

If possible, take some time even if it's only once a month to have one to one time with the sibling who isn't getting as much attention. Think about an activity that they would particularly enjoy, as often family outings are dominated by the obsessions or fears of the child with autism. Take time to acknowledge the feelings of a child whose sibling may be aggressive. They may not feel able to have friends come to visit, may not get that bedtime story they wanted or help with their homework. They may not get the chance to talk to you about something that's troubling them because of their sibling with autism. It's a balancing act but being aware can help to make positive outcomes for everyone. If possible try to identify an activity that both children may enjoy together, to get them to work together and slowly find some common ground to form a bond.

Facial expressions – People on the autistic spectrum have difficulty in reading facial expressions, body language and interpreting the emotions another person is feeling and portraying. Communication is much more than just verbal, and this is what can make interacting with others so difficult for those with autism. Research has found that this inability actually gets worse over time.

From a young age it can help to turn this into a game. Try making different facial expressions and get your child to guess which emotion you're feeling. If your child is able to do this, then you can build on their skills by taking turns and letting them make the faces.

Memory – Children with autism can have problems with their short-term memory. They can remember everything that happened on the day they met their favourite YouTuber and what they ate for lunch on that day four years ago, but they can't remember what they had for breakfast this morning. Understanding that this is an autistic trait has helped me with my frustration when my son can't remember every night that he needs to put his socks in the laundry basket every night. Playing games such as matching pairs can help a child's recall.

Immunity – School absences can be fairly frequent for a lot of children on the spectrum, as they can have low immunity and catch every bug going. Research has shown that significant numbers of those with autism have dysfunction of the immune system. Restricted diets may not help with this and so vitamin supplements may help support their immune system.

Gastrointestinal problems – There is a known link between autism and gastrointestinal problems. Constipation is common in children with autism and high levels of anxiety can cause stomach aches and irritable bowel syndrome. Children on the spectrum are also six times more likely than TD peers to have food allergies and sensitivities. If you notice symptoms in your child, it may be useful to keep a diary to see if there is a pattern emerging of when it occurs, such as just before school or just after eating tomatoes etc. Talk to your GP if you are concerned.

Stripping it back – Sometimes it feels like your children can take two steps forward and then three steps back. If something stops working, then you may need to go back a few steps and start over again. For instance, we were on holiday recently and my daughter was lying in bed one morning when my husband asked her if she wanted bacon for breakfast. She started crying, threw the duvet over her head and wouldn't speak. It took a few minutes to realise that asking her if she wanted bacon was making a presumption that she would be eating, and her PDA was making her feel anxious at the loss of control. Instead we had to ask her if she wanted something to eat and then wait for her response before giving her options of what she would like to eat. The lack of normal routine because we were on holiday had triggered her anxiety and she needed to feel a sense of control. It might not be immediately obvious what the cause of a child's behaviour might be but being a detective and unpicking the problem can help to find out the cause and implement strategies.

Sugar – Children on the spectrum can have problems absorbing sugar. I remember taking my son to a service at his school's church and halfway through they handed out chocolate coins to the children. I had no idea the effect that a simple chocolate coin could have on a five-year-old child. We had to leave early because his whole demeanour completely changed. His beautiful blue eyes suddenly went completely black and he was just so full of rage and anger. When we got home he stormed up to his bedroom and started smashing anything he could reach, I had never seen him do this before.

Similarly, white icing on a slice of birthday cake had the same devastating effect. Another time he secretly ate a whole bag of sweets to himself and I turned around to find him collapsed on a sofa in M&S, completely spaced out, shaking and feeling sick. Each time that he had sugar overload we gave him pasta which immediately counteracted the sugar effect. We now have to ration sugar intake and avoid it where possible and it's something we have to be very aware of, especially at parties.

Risk of depression, self-harm and schizophrenia - Anxiety and depression are more common in autistic people, with a fifty three percent lifetime rate of mood disorders and fifty percent lifetime rate of anxiety in autistic adults; it is therefore no surprise that links with mental health problems can be common.

The level of help you can get from services such as CAMHS, can vary greatly depending on where in the UK you live. If you talk to anyone about CAMHS referrals now, you will hear the word 'thresholds'. Eight years ago, my son was seen by CAMHS because he was generally anxious. Recently, my daughter was suffering crippling anxiety which was affecting all aspect of her life and yet her referral was rejected, and we were told that her new school had to deal with the situation. My son was feeling suicidal and we couldn't get him a CAMHS appointment because he hadn't actively attempted it. It can be a terrifying subject to deal with your child's mental health issues, but If you have concerns over your child's low mood seek professional help as soon as possible. You may be able to get a CAMHS referral to help with therapies and interventions or at the very least get signposted towards charities and organisations that may be able to help.

Fidgeting – Some schools are opposed to children bringing in 'fiddle toys' especially if you mention the dreaded words 'fidget spinner.' The fidget spinner was a classic example of a tool designed for children with special needs that became popular with all children and due to being used inappropriately in the classroom, it ruined it for everyone and they became banned. In one school I worked at they wouldn't even let me use a fidget spinner in a therapy room because they weren't even allowed on the premises.

Fortunately, most schools do recognise the benefits of giving a child a fiddle toy, to keep them focused and calm. There are many various types, some of which are attached to key rings, ensuring that the child doesn't lose the toy. Popular ones are small soft stress relieving objects that fit in one hand. Wind-up toys are not appropriate as they will be too distracting for the rest of the class but can work well for outside of school.

Children can use fidgeting or playing with someone's hair or a toy as a way of self-regulating their emotions, especially in stressful situations. Unless a child is being inappropriate or hurting themselves or others then consider whether you want to stop them from fidgeting. If you stop one regulating behaviour, they may exchange it for another which is less socially acceptable or could lose their temper because they have lost their strategy for remaining calm.

Mental Health - Some children may not always simply have autism. There are comorbid conditions that can combine with autism and can share core traits. PDA, ADHD, Dyspraxia, anxiety, Obsessive Compulsive Disorder (OCD) to name but a few, can be common in a person with autism.

If there are traits in your child that don't seem to fit the standard autistic traits, it may be worth considering if there are other factors at work and speaking to the class teacher, SENDCo or GP.

Research has shown that how a child perceives their diagnosis can have a direct effect on their mental health. If they are encouraged to see their diagnosis in a positive way it will help their resilience and their willingness to participate in interventions and joining groups of autistic peers. Reducing the perceived stigma of being someone with autism is vital for future mental wellbeing and this is just as important at school as at home. Children role model the actions of adults and the behaviours of adult school staff need to be open and inclusive at all times.

Unfortunately, as a parent of a child on the autistic spectrum you may be a frequent visitor to CAMHS, GPs and Paediatricians as our children are more likely to experience mental health problems over their lifetime, especially anxiety disorders. Early interventions can have a positive effect and so communication with your child and relevant professionals are vital.

Transgender – Research suggests that there is a link between autism and gender dysphoria. Some people that want to transition may find obstacles as professionals can often view it as being a part of their autism and are reluctant to let the person start the transition process and dismiss their wishes. There are varying suggestions as to why children on the spectrum are almost eight percent more likely to experience gender dysphoria and the conversation continues between academics. No one chooses to have gender dysphoria in the same way that you cannot choose to have autism and listening to your child about any subject that affects their mental health is a positive step.

OCD – Obsessive Compulsive Disorder can affect children with autism. In a world that seems out of control and full of anxiety, the overwhelming compulsion to control one aspect of life is unsurprising. My daughter has OCD, in her case, she has a constant need to wash her hands. She is only eight years old but has already stopped being friends with a classmate she had known for years, because she witnessed him walking out of the school toilets without washing his hands. There was absolutely nothing this little boy could say that would redeem himself in her eyes, it was an absolute deal breaker. Fortunately, the school have been very understanding and accommodating of her needs and have allowed her to keep cleaning items in her drawer that she can access at any time.

   For children that have OCD and feel the need to keep washing their hands during the school day, which can be disruptive to learning, small bottles of hand gel in their bag or packs of baby wipes can be helpful if the school agree. The child can keep them in their drawer and use them when needed, without having to keep leaving the classroom.

Continence – Because children on the spectrum can have difficulty in processing the signals from their body it is no surprise that continence issues can arise. Both of my children are completely unaware that they need to go to the toilet until the very last minute when it's almost too late. Most of the time it's because they're so engrossed in a game that they don't realise and then all of a sudden, they just run and if there's already someone on the toilet or the dog is sat on the stairs in their way then it often results in an accident.

   Both children take a spare pair of underwear, a plastic bag and a pair of spare trousers in their backpacks and if they have an accident at school they discretely deal with it without their classmates realising.

We can sometimes tell that they need to go to the toilet because they unconsciously start doing what we refer to as the 'jiggle dance.' Even at this point they still don't realise that they need to go, and they can become quite defensive because we can see the signals that they're not picking up on.

If your child is having issues with continence, remember it's not something they choose and making them anxious is only going to make the problem worse. Stay calm and assure them that these things happen and don't make an issue out of it. Talk to them about what happened and why, and if it does become a problem then seek professional help. For older children, the website ERIC is a great website that helps children and parents with bedwetting and continence issues.

Soiling themselves is common in children on the autistic spectrum. One reason for continence problems can be the child's restrictive diet, leading to constipation. When a child is constipated liquid faeces and seep past the blockage and leak into pants and even clothing. If constipation is a problem, then more fluids and high fibre foods need to be introduced into the diet.

When a child does manage to recognise the signals and use the toilet appropriately, use rewards like stickers or tokens to motivate them. If they refuse to use the toilet because of fear of being in the bathroom for example, then gradually introduce them to the bathroom and talk about what interests them and take away the pressure of thinking about using the toilet. Overtime they will become more used to being in the room and their anxiety should reduce.

Anxiety – Autism and anxiety are closely linked. For a person who has no idea what someone else is thinking or feeling, it is no surprise that they might feel anxious. The many causes and triggers of anxiety can be complex to unravel. There are various types of anxiety disorders that a child on the spectrum may present with. Generalised Anxiety Disorder (GAD) is characterised by irrational fears and worrying about something that may or may not even happen. Overthinking things and worrying can be common to children with autism. Social Anxiety Disorder (SAD) means that the child is terrified of saying or doing something that will humiliate themselves in front of others. These children are excessively shy and self-conscious. Separation Anxiety is more common in younger children and is characterised by children who are anxious and clingy when having to leave their parents. If a child's anxiety interferes with their daily life and continues for a long time, then professional help should be sought, and the first step would be your GP.

Motor skills – Movement, co-ordination, motor skills, correct posture and walking can be lacking in children with autism and the greater their motor skills difficulties, the greater the social communication difficulties they may also experience. Practice can improve these skills, something as simple as regularly playing catch with a ball can help improve co-ordination. Occupational Therapy can help with issues such as walking, posture and how to hold a pen, so talk to the school if you think your child needs further help with their motor skills.

If you close your eyes and stretch your arms as wide as you can you are still aware of where your arms and hands are. However, children with autism don't always have this natural ability. I have seen children on the spectrum get told off time and again for barging past people, especially in a line of children at school. The child then gets defensive and upset, because they weren't aware that they were doing anything wrong and can make matters worse by lashing out in temper. Their spacial awareness is reduced and understanding and patience can help them understand that they need to be hyper aware of their body, especially when around other people.

Sensitivity – Children on the spectrum can be hyper or hypo sensitive at different times. Often the environment they are in can be overwhelming and cause anxiety, so it helps to be able to recognise the triggers in your child to avoid a meltdown or complete shutdown of the senses.

When my children decided that they wanted to go to their first theme park and to stay over in the heavily themed onsite hotel, we approached this in stages. First, we visited the park for the day, then a few months later when the park was closed for the winter we spent a night in the hotel. When the park re-opened we finally did everything together and had a fun day followed by a night in the hotel. It allowed them to deal with each overwhelming part of the trip individually, so that it all ran smoothly when we attempted the trip in full.

For children who have oversensitivity to sound, trips to concerts or simply using hand driers in public toilets can be almost impossible. Ear defenders are available online and can be very effective at allowing children to participate in family or peer activities without causing anxiety, they even come in a range of attractive colours.

Weighted blankets are popular amongst those children who are hypo sensitive and need a greater amount of pressure in order to feel comfortable. One child I worked with said it best "they're like having a cuddle, without having to deal with people touching you." Some children on the spectrum particularly like the feeling of suppression, the pressure is enjoyable to them and makes them feel safe. Some children don't like them as they feel overheated. However, on the whole, they are very popular amongst children on the spectrum.

Weighted jackets/waistcoats are also available online and are often recommended by Occupational Therapists to reduce hyperactivity and to aid focus and attention. They are said to have a calming effect and are popular and practical.

Hyper sensitivity of the senses can be over-whelming and children may need help in managing this by finding somewhere quiet, unstimulating to regulate their emotions. Children with hypo sensitivity can actively seek noise and need help to find stimulation.

For children who have issues with getting ready for school because of sock seams and scratchy labels, Marks and Spencer now have a range of autism friendly school clothing.

Creative writing – Abstract thought can unsurprisingly be challenging for some children who have a very literal understanding of the world. Some children on the spectrum can be creative and can write pieces at school with no problems, but for some children this is almost impossible.

Where appropriate, it would be helpful for the class teacher to link a story the child needs to write, to one of their obsessions. My son struggled to write the first sentence of a story, yet when he was asked to write about Sonic the Hedgehog, they couldn't stop him from writing pages. Practice and patience will help, linking writing to their likes will motivate them and making up silly stories when they're bored in the car or walking to school will help them to start thinking creatively.

Avoiding Touch – Children with autism can be hypersensitive to touch. This inability to tolerate being touched or cuddled by others can be difficult for the parents or siblings. I have heard many mothers in particular explaining to me that they struggled to bond with their child because they felt their child didn't love or even like them. It is important not to force or coerce a child into something they are not comfortable with. It is always thoughtful to ask first if they want a hug and to ensure family members and friends don't just hug or touch the child without thinking. Over time, what a child can or cannot cope with may change and they may be able to tolerate being gently hugged, don't take it personally. Your child's ability to tolerate touch in no way reflects their emotions or feelings towards you, it is a sensory issue.

Emotions – Some children with autism are unable to understand their own emotions, they may not respond in a typical way and might display their emotions differently to others. A good way of helping a child to understand and verbalise their emotions are scaling tools. There are many different types available online which can be used from an early age upwards. Blob Trees are popular and depict little blob people displaying various emotions. I have tried this with children aged four and they understood the concept easily when I asked them to colour in the blob person that they thought was most like them; even though they may not have been able to verbalise their feelings. There are others which show various Lego people displaying different emotions. I use a Minecraft one which says things like 'I feel like an Enderman and want to teleport when people look at me' or 'I feel like a Creeper and I want to explode' this one has so far proved to be the most popular in the schools I've worked in.

The most well-known is the Incredible Five Point Scale with an accompanying book. Flash cards can also be useful, or for some children the film Inside Out has been helpful in explaining emotions and how the brain works. It has been a great way of starting conversations about how they feel and explaining that we need a little sadness, anger and fear as well as joy and that one emotion might not always be in control all of the time.

Conversations – Even when a child is able to communicate verbally, it can still be very difficult for those on the spectrum to participate in a conversation. Tone of voice and facial expressions can be hard to read and the person with autism can find it difficult to know when it's their turn to speak.

My son once explained to me why he never replied when an adult said hello to him. He said that it was like trying to make conversation in a foreign language. He said "imagine the only word you know in French is bonjour and when you go to France, someone says bonjour to you and you answer by saying bonjour too. As soon as you respond in French they think you know their language and then all of a sudden, they start talking to you in French and then you feel embarrassed and confused and don't know what to say. I don't want that to happen, so I just ignore people when they speak to me." I thought this was a really insightful way to explain why he kept blanking people when they spoke to him and was a perfect way of explaining what he was scared of. I hadn't really appreciated before how much of outsider he felt in his own life which was a sobering thought. Practising conversations can be helpful so that talking to others isn't such an abstract and scary thought, however this may take time. My son is thirteen now and although he will sometimes answer someone that talks to him, he tries to only shop on places that have a self-service point, so that he doesn't need to interact with anyone.

Intonation is something that children on the spectrum can also have problems with. If you cannot understand tone, it is difficult to understand what is meant by the other person. For instance, think of the sentence 'I didn't say she murdered her husband' and then repeat it, emphasising a different word each time.

I didn't say she murdered her husband.

I **didn't** say she murdered her husband.

I didn't **say** she murdered her husband.

I didn't say **she** murdered her husband.

I didn't say she **murdered** her husband.

I didn't say she murdered **her** husband.

I didn't say she murdered her **husband.**

Emphasising one particular word at a time, changes the whole context of what is being said. This example shows the confusion children on the spectrum can experience.

Picture Exchange Communication System – (PECS) was originally created as a tool to help non-verbal children with autism communicate with others. Most schools have PECS cards that they use, sets can be ordered pretty inexpensively online or are even free on some websites.

Depending where on the autistic spectrum a child is, has an impact on their speech. Aspie's are usually quite verbal, however towards the other end of the spectrum some children are non-verbal or even pre-verbal. Anger and frustration are not surprising for a child who can't verbalise what they want to say, or interact with adults, nursery/school staff and their peers. These feelings of frustration can frequently result in behavioural problems and physical aggression and PECS can be useful at reducing these emotions.

It can be fun and empowering for the child to take photographs of what they want to be used on the cards. If they feel involved in the process, they will be more motivated to use the PECS. Be aware of possible problems due to the autistic trait of literal thinking. For example, sets can show a plate with cutlery on a card depicting lunch. This may work okay if the child is having school dinners, however I've known children have a complete meltdown because they have packed lunch and so the card was wrong and didn't depict what it was meant to represent. Another child I knew began screaming on certain days when he went home, it took a long time to work out that the problem was down to the picture the school was using for home. The child had taken the photo themselves and in picture was his dad's car. Because of this, the child expected the car to be there every day and when it wasn't because Dad worked shifts, it prompted severe meltdowns as the image on the PECS card didn't match the one at home.

Being mindful of how children with autism struggle to cope with something being different or vague. PECS images may need to be chosen with great care and if the child is not responding well to them, you may need to play detective to find out what is causing the upset and anxiety as it may be something that could easily be changed to make the child happier.

Selective Mutism – A lot of children with autism can be selectively mute, particularly girls. The term 'selective' mutism doesn't sit comfortably with me because if you didn't know anything about this condition it might lead you to believe that the child has some control over their speech and this is definitely not the case. It's called selective because it won't be apparent in all environments, not that it happens through choice. Commonly, children will be able to converse normally at home, but when they are in school or for instance a doctor's appointment then their heightened level of anxiety prevents them from being able to talk. Especially in KS1 at school, there is usually a focus on reading during the school day which might be with the class teacher, a teaching assistant or possibly a volunteer. When the children are assessed in their reading they can then progress onto a higher level, but this is difficult when your child is selectively mute at school.

I worked with one child who would not speak at all if there were any adult school staff around to hear them. The children reliably informed me that she would laugh and giggle with them when there were no adults around, but not one member of staff had ever heard her talk. Her mum came into school one morning and told me that she had been in a local shop with her daughter and they were talking together quite happily, until her daughter turned around and saw one of the school teaching assistants behind her in the queue and instantly was unable to talk.

It was so sad to think about this poor little girl spending all day so anxious that she couldn't communicate. Speech and Language therapy can possibly help some children, PECS cards can also be of use if the child is willing to use them. If your child has selective mutism, then don't pressure them to speak or make a huge deal out of it if they do. I worked in one school where a child with this condition suddenly spoke in class and the kids all went quiet and the teacher started shouting "well done, well done, you spoke." They all clapped her and then gave her a worker of the week certificate and as a consequence, the distressed little girl never spoke in school again.

Some children do grow out of severe selective mutism. When they start secondary school, they can suddenly start talking, because they connect the mutism to their primary school.

Although the mutism might seem to disappear, it can reoccur, especially in times of stress. If you are concerned about your child talk to the school or your GP for referrals to access help.

Echolalia – Echolalia is very common in children with autism, up to seventy five percent of people on the spectrum have displayed echolalia. It is the repetition of something someone else has said, which can be directly spoken to the child, or even lines or whole scenes from a film or TV programme.

It is considered to be a positive development of language in children with autism and should not be discouraged. As well as the practical aspect of speech development, children on the spectrum find comfort in repetition and hearing words over and over again, it is the reason why they will repeatedly ask the same question.

Stimming – Stimming is the repetition of sounds, movements such as flapping of hands or repetitive movement of objects. This can often be seen as a negative behaviour particularly in schools where it can be seen as a distraction to the rest of the class. However, it is a self-regulating behaviour and offers the child relief. If a child is prevented from stimming this may result in far more negative behaviours such as aggressiveness.

Happiness – I once worked in my son's primary school as a teaching assistant. Every morning at play time when I was supervising my class, I was able to see across to the upper school playground and could observe my son. Every day I would watch him playing all by himself and every day it hurt beyond belief. I only worked mornings and so at the end of each school day I would question him about what friends he had played with. Every day the answer would be the same, "I played on my own." I tried to encourage him to join games that he wasn't interested in just to be social and I spoke to the class teacher about my concerns. The school was helpful and set up a buddy system, so that he would have a friend to play with.

The buddy system didn't work because my son refused to participate. I naively assumed that all of the children that he had randomly been assigned to a class with, were his friends. At the very least he thought of them as acquaintances and excepting two or three of them, he even considered them to be annoying.

One day when I was driving him home from school, trying to talk about friends without desperation in my voice, he said to me "you always asked me who I played with at play time, but you never ask me was I happy?" This made me pause, and once again this little boy proved that he was far more perceptive than his poor stressed mother. He told me that he was happy being by himself at play time and so I stopped asking.

I never fully appreciated his point of view until I went to an autism seminar and one of the speakers talked about the meaning of being happy. For those without autism, being happy often means the inclusion of others, such as meeting up with their friends. Children on the spectrum were more commonly happy when they were alone and indulging in solitary pursuits such as reading, gaming or drawing. Taking away the anxiety of interacting with others allowed the person with autism to relax.

Each person with autism is completely different and some may desperately want to play with their classmates. Different schools have different strategies for playground inclusion, including friendship benches so that if someone is feeling lonely they can sit on the bench and peers can come and play with them. If your child is upset about not having anyone to play with, then speak to the school to see what they can do to encourage peer friendships.

Obsessions – It will probably come as no surprise that obsessions are included in this list of behaviours you may be presented with. Obsessions can be both positive and negative but are generally all consuming.

Whenever I've heard people discussing autism and obsessions, trains are usually mentioned. It's true that there are many children on the spectrum who are obsessive about trains, or can memorise train tables or stations, but this is clearly not true of everyone. I attended an autism conference where it was stated that parents and professionals should never use a child's obsession as a bargaining tool. It is tempting to use the one thing they love as leverage for good behaviour, but this can have a detrimental impact. Obsessions are not a passing fancy, they are used by the child for self-regulation, consistency and relaxation when dealing with a world they may struggle to cope with. Removing their obsession, is counter-productive as this could then cause further negative behaviour that you're trying to reduce.

Obsessions can be a good way of bonding with your child, such as starting conversations or enjoying days out themed around whatever the child is interested in. A child's obsession may be the only thing they have that relaxes them and where possible, shouldn't be withheld.

Eye Contact – Over the years I have seen many professionals, especially in the school environment shouting in the face of a child with autism telling them to look them in the eye. THIS SHOULD NEVER BE DONE! Those on the spectrum can find the intimacy of eye contact uncomfortable and even physically painful. Those without autism wrongly presume that if a child is not looking directly at them, they are not listening to them. It depends really on what the person is trying to achieve. Do they want the child to look at them or listen to them? A child with autism may rarely do both. If you do manage to force a child on the spectrum to look at you without them being uncomfortable, they will most probably be counting your eyelashes or wondering why one eyebrow is higher than the other and concentrating on other details than what is being said. Forcing a child with autism to make contact is an outdated and often cruel approach and should not be insisted upon.

Repetition – Children on the spectrum enjoy repetition of all kinds. When my son was two he was obsessed by the Take That song 'Shine', we were driving to the coast for a holiday and for the full one hundred and five miles of the journey, he made us play that song over and over again, back to back. By the end of the trip, he was really happy and calm, but my husband and I never wanted to hear the song EVER again. Some children like to hear phrases repeated over and over, whilst others like to watch the same TV programme or DVD over and over again and their enjoyment is no different to the very first time they ever saw it. Other children may enjoy watching a toy spinning over and over again. Repetition is an emotional regulator and can be a positive way to feel a sense of consistency and control and where possible should be supported.

Explaining protection – It can be a tricky balancing act, trying to explain to a potentially vulnerable child how to protect themselves in terms that they will understand, without frightening them. The NSPCC website has useful tips how to do on this. The best is their Pants Song, which uses an animated child-friendly video and song to explain to children that there are parts of their body that are private. It has a very catchy song which helps to put the point across in a non-threatening way that kids enjoy.

For older children there is a great video on YouTube about consent using the analogy of making a cup of tea for someone to explain the concept of consent. If you do show this to your child, make sure you use the clean version or the British VO version, as the normal one has some strong swearing in. It might be worth watching it yourself first so that you can judge whether it is appropriate.

Teenagers – There are two milestones in every child's life that brings fear into the heart of their parents and they are the 'terrible twos' and 'the teenage years.'

Thankfully the terrible twos only last for one year, unfortunately however the teenage years can last for what may seem like years. I heard an analogy once that adolescence is like your child has been put into a rocket flying around the moon. They get farther and farther away, before going completely out of radio range altogether and suddenly you can't communicate with them at all. When you've finally given up home, you suddenly get a faint signal that proves they're coming back to you.

Adolescence is a difficult time for any young person, so it's even harder when you add autism into the mix too. In basic terms, the problem is that the part of the brain that deals with logic and reasoning gets closed down for refurbishment and expansion and so everything is routed through the amygdala. The amygdala is the primitive part of the brain and is where the 'fight, flight or freeze' response comes from. Anything that is said to a teenager is processed through this part of the brain which can account for the defensive attitude you may get confronted with and the feeling that you have to walk on eggshells for fear of upsetting them.

These changes in the brain also makes the teenager prone to risky behaviours. Stay as calm and patient as you can, especially when they accuse you of not knowing what it was like to be a teenager, as if you were actually born in your forties and never went through the pain of adolescence. If they need extra support then consider talking to their school, your GP or a local charity that can offer counselling.

Troubleshooting and Strategies

Resilience – Children on the spectrum can be vulnerable and as a young child with a disability they can be considered 'at risk.' The best way of counteracting the risks they face is by teaching resilience. The word 'resilience' can seem a little abstract, but it can make a huge difference to those with autism. I have seen first-hand the difference resilience made in my own son. Previously he would be crushed by a harsh word, or something going wrong and it would seem like the end of the world. Since his school provided him with resilience interventions, he has been able to shrug off the setbacks far easier than he did before. Resilience is all about raising confidence and promoting independence. Mindfulness can also help with resilience, if you think your child might benefit from learning resilience speak to the school SENDCo to see if that is something the school can help with.

Encouraging positive behaviour - Rewarding good behaviour through the use of a sticker chart is a popular and often effective way of motivating a child to continue to exhibit positive behaviours. Children on the autistic spectrum can find it difficult to wait for the reward and can struggle with abstract notions, so rewards have to be achievable and not take too long to reach.

You can tailor a reward chart, by making the rewards specific to the child's interests and it may be possible to get the school onboard. Try asking the class teacher to let you know at the end of the day whether your child earned rewards points for their chart by reaching an agreed behaviour target.

Even from a young age, my son has always been motivated by money. We told him that he would earn two pounds for every school day that he behaved well, but that he wouldn't earn any if there were reports of negative behaviour from the teacher. During the first week of trying this new approach, the teacher commented on how my son's behaviour was suddenly markedly improved. We started using this five years ago and the system is still working well, he still has his off days as it's not totally in his control, but for the most part it has been a benefit.

For other children it may be a day out that motivates them or a small toy or game, for others the reward chart is too abstract and in the moment of anxiety or anger they cannot help themselves and react negatively. Reward charts may lose their effectiveness, or may become effective as a child gets older, so it's trial and error and having strategies at your disposal when needed. You can always reintroduce a reward chart, if a child suddenly needs a little motivation.

Keeping it simple – Children on the spectrum take longer to process what is said to them and can become easily overwhelmed by too much information in a short space of time. Try to keep communication to a minimum if the child is struggling to understand or focus.

Keep sentences short, don't use twenty words when four would do. Keep language simple, clear and factual. Children on the spectrum do not understand vague language. My daughter gets particularly frustrated with me, when I answer a question with "mmm," she shouts at me "what does mmm mean? Mmm means nothing. Just say yes or no." Before she began getting irritated with me, I never had any idea that I didn't really answer questions properly. In my head I meant yes but was often distracted with one thing or another and never really thought about what I was saying. Always use your child's name before you start speaking if you think that they may not be listening.

Instructions – As mentioned, children can find it hard to focus and remember instructions. If you are asking a child on the spectrum to follow instructions, where possible try to only give them one at a time. I have worked with several children who could only retain one to two instructions at a time, any more than this would result in either a meltdown or the child completely forgetting all of what they had been asked to do and. To make matters worse, they're then faced with a teacher or teaching assistant upset at them because they didn't do what had been asked of them and failed to   follow the rules.

My son once got told off by a teacher who had told him to 'pull his socks up.' My son was clearly confused but not wanting to get in trouble did as he was told and physically pulled his socks up. His classmates all started laughing, which made him even more confused and upset. The teacher was absolutely incensed by what he perceived as insolent behaviour and gave my bewildered and hurt son a detention. This teacher knew that my son had Asperger's Syndrome and yet seemed blissfully unaware of common traits such as literal understanding. When talking to children on the spectrum, especially when giving them instructions ensure that you don't use metaphors like 'he hit the roof' etc, as this can be confusing. Be literal in your communication and don't use ambiguity such as 'we'll see' or 'maybe later' although this may take a bit of practice.

41

Worry box – Some children who suffer with anxiety can find dream catchers useful, they are after all pretty and the child's belief that it will catch their bad dreams or fears whilst they sleep may be very beneficial. For others, a worry box might be of use. When I've prepared these for children in the past, we have decorated a cardboard box about the size of a shoebox with colourful paper and stickers and put a label on the top, naming it as a 'Worry Box.' The idea is to put a slit in the top so that the box acts as a post box. The child writes down something they are worried about and then places the piece of paper into the worry box. The child needs to be assured that no one else is going to look at what they have written and that once the worry has been posted, the box takes away the worry for them.

Getting their attention – I've seen a lot of adults start talking to a child only to get cross because they've received no response and the child hasn't listened to them. I remember a time when my son and I were alone in the house, I talking to him and he didn't answer. I asked him why he hadn't responded, and he said, "because I didn't realise you were talking to me." I laughed at him and said "but we're the only ones here. Who did you think I was talking to?" He looked confused and didn't have a response, he hadn't even realised that we were the only two people in the house. It was a good lesson for me to understand that although it was obvious to me that I was talking to him, it wasn't obvious to him. Try using their name at the beginning of the sentence, if you are expecting them to listen.

Mindfulness – Recently, more and more people are embracing the benefits of mindfulness. For those not in the know, it's basically about taking the time to stop and learn how to just be in the moment. It can be quite therapeutic to block out everything else and focus on one thing, like a seashell for example, or to concentrate on what is happening in your own body.

Meditation and mindfulness can help benefit a child's mental wellbeing and the positives of this reach into all areas of a child's life. It can also improve their attention and focus and find inner peace.

To properly teach children mindfulness there are trained professionals whose services are usually bought in by schools, or there are local kids clubs that run sessions. However, there are lots of examples online of activities you can try with your child if you think they might benefit from a little calming time. You don't need any fancy or expensive equipment to practice, all you need is a quiet space. One simple exercise you could begin with, is having your child lie down with their eyes closed and then slowly and methodically talking them through the various parts of the body, beginning at the toes up to the head. Ask them to focus on the relevant body part as you mention them and then ask them to notice the feel the ground beneath, the location of any pressure points, feel the blood rushing through the body etc.

Another example is to get them to hold a seashell or a teddy bear and close their eyes, ask them to think about the texture, the temperature, the colour, the shape, how it makes them feel etc.

Tone of Voice – It can be difficult when you are angry, irritated, tired or anxious yourself to keep a calm and even tone when talking to a child. You may have not even realised that you raised your voice, but a child with autism will reflect this in their interaction with you and a simple conversation can quickly escalate into a full-blown argument. It can take practice but being aware of your own tone of voice and body language will have an effect on your child's response to you and others.

Stay positive – This can be quite difficult but try to be positive in your language as children are more likely to remember the negative words. This is not something that is solely an autism trait and is useful for all children. Instead of saying "don't run," try praising them by saying "good walking" instead. Emphasising the positive and praising the good behaviour will give the child higher levels of self-esteem. In the same way, try to ignore negative behaviour unless they are hurting themselves or others and only reward positive behaviours.

Understanding – Do not simply assume that because your child may have been looking in your direction, or perhaps even nodded that they actually understood what you have said. Check that they have understood by asking them to repeat what you said to them.

Give them time and space to calm down – In a world where everything moves at such a fast pace making time to be calm isn't always possible. Children on the spectrum need to have time to reflect and regulate their emotions. After a meltdown it is essential for a child to calm down, whether in school or at home it can be helpful to have a safe space where the child knows that they can go and be by themselves. It is important that this is not seen as a place of punishment or somewhere to have time out because they've done something wrong.

Using the word finish – If a child gets upset at having to end a particularly enjoyable activity, such as playing on the computer, you could try using a visual timer such as one with traffic light colours or verbal cues to let them know that the activity will be ending soon. When it is time to stop what they are doing, children on the spectrum respond better to the word 'finish' rather than 'stop.' Using the word stop has negative connotations and may insinuate that they are doing something wrong. The word finish is a much more positive and less confrontational word.

Social stories – It's difficult to speak to any autism professional without hearing the words 'social stories,' yet so many parents aren't aware of exactly what they are and how they are of help, even though they've been in use for almost thirty years. These sequential stories are effective for any event that may need visual explanation, such as brushing teeth, a visit to the dentist, transitioning from one class, or school to another. Social stories are useful for helping a child to process something that has happened, or to be prepared for something that is yet to happen. You can do them quite easily by dividing the event into steps and there's no requirement to have any artistic skill, stick men will do perfectly well as there is not too much detail for the children to absorb. Social stories are popular despite lack of in-depth research into their effectiveness. My children have used them at school and they have worked wonders. There are books about social stories available online and you can talk to your child's school to see if they have any tips, or if they are currently use social stories for your child and if they work.

Now and then board – Children on the spectrum can have difficulties in understanding time. If an adult in school says to a child "we're going to go to assembly, then we're doing English and then it's playtime." The child may not be able to listen and comprehend so many words in one go. They will more than likely latch onto the one word that interests them, which in this case would be 'playtime.' The child is then going to get upset because you said playtime, yet you're not letting them go out to play immediately. In these instances, shortened visual timetables are useful. It is simply a board separated by a vertical line in the middle with the word 'now' written on the left-hand side and 'next' written at the top of the right-hand column and a picture beneath each word to signify what is going to happen and in what order.

Toothbrushes – Brushing their teeth can be particularly difficult for children on the autistic spectrum. Mornings can be a time full of demands and are flashpoints for meltdowns so brushing your teeth is unsurprisingly a trigger for anger and anxiety. For my son, he has never been able to get used to the pain of the brush along his gums, particularly when he was in the process of losing one of his baby teeth and his mouth was already hurting him so much.

The other problem we experienced was the taste of toothpaste. He's thirteen years old now and he still can't brush his teeth before he eats breakfast because of the minty taste that the brushing leaves in his mouth. I've lost count of the amount of time he lost at school when he was in Reception and Years One and Two due to vomiting on the journey to school because the mint taste made him feel physically sick.

Three sided toothbrushes with soft bristles are available online and work well for those with autism. Thankfully you can also buy unflavoured toothpaste which can help make toothbrushing a less stressful event for both children and parents. I just wish I'd known about them nine years ago.

Radar key – No doubt on your way to use public toilets, you've been met with a sign that says, 'Radar keys only' and probably thought that when your child gets a diagnosis and they join the 'disability club' they will be formally presented with the mythical radar key (at least that was my thinking). This isn't the case, you can buy them at any time.

My daughter was unable to use public toilets because of the noise of the hand driers and it was awful to see her distress, even using ear defenders didn't really help. We went online and simply bought a radar key, which cost around two pounds. My little girl had a diagnosis, but I didn't need to prove it in order to purchase a key. It has been so helpful having a radar key, especially as my children can't wait in a long queue, when they need to go, they need to go. There are several online sites that sell them.

Therapies – In schools, children will now regularly receive interventions and types of therapy if needed from trained teaching assistants or trained professionals. Cognitive Behavioural Therapy (CBT) can be very effective for children with autism. It is a popular form of therapy as it identifies the cycles of thoughts that cause ongoing anxiety and helps to prevent the negative thoughts that continue the cycle. Forest school, drama, music and art therapy are also popular and effective and engaging for the children. Ask your child's class teacher or SENDCo if you are interested in any opportunities for appropriate support that the school can offer your child.

Lego Therapy – Lego Therapy was literally made for children with autism. It was created by Daniel Legoff as a response to children on the spectrum being reluctant to engage in intervention therapies. Lego bricks are colourful and can be built or taken apart just as easily, thereby avoiding a meltdown and children on the spectrum appear particularly drawn to Lego. There are infinite things to build which can spark their creativity, alternatively for those that like structure there are easy to follow instructions. I have led Lego Therapy groups in mainstream schools and have seen first-hand the positive effect it can have on a child's ability to focus, verbalise and interact with their peers. The therapy takes place with three participants who are each assigned a role such as builder, engineer and supplier and work together to build a specific model, following their specific role. Schools often have their own sets and provide Lego Therapy interventions, or if this is too structured then local groups can offer Lego clubs for children on the spectrum to play with their peers. There is also a book about Lego Therapy by Daniel Legoff for those interested in finding out more or running a session themselves.

Routines – Children on the autistic spectrum generally love routines. Routines give them comfort and consistency. My son would regularly end up with a CAMHS referral at the beginning of the summer because he couldn't cope with the change in routine. After the hibernation of the winter months, we would take advantage of the better weather at the weekends and take the kids out to lots of different places. I wanted to try and give my children as many different experiences as possible and it took me a couple of years of this backfiring before I realised the cause of my son's anxieties, it was the fear of the unknown. Once we knew that he was struggling with the unpredictability of the weekends, we were able to help him. We gave him visual time tables, so he would know what was going to happen on the day out and we downloaded an app onto his tablet that allowed him to track our car journey. He could see our home location and our destination points and finally felt a sense of control.

It is possible to make changes easier for a child to manage, but where possible routines should be followed; morning and bedtime routines are especially important.

Savant super powers – It is a myth that all children with Asperger's have special abilities such as instantly knowing the amount of straws spilled onto a table. There are obviously children who are geniuses and can play piano concertos at the age of three, but it is not common.

My son could read Harry Potter at the age of four, but he also walked into doors and couldn't zip up his own coat. I have met parents who were worried that their children didn't possess any special gifts. If you do have a mini Mensa member on your hands then encourage it, but if you don't that's perfectly normal.

Pets– There is a great deal of academic research around the positive effects that animals have on autistic children, particularly dogs and horses. I am particularly interested in this subject as I have seen first-hand the effects of a therapy dog on my children. My daughter had begged for a puppy for years, but my son had never been an animal person and didn't want the tie of having a dog. Eventually, as they began to dislike long car journeys and we were going out less and less, we made the decision to buy a puppy. We did our research about which breed would be best for us and finally purchased a goldendoodle (a golden retriever and a standard poodle mix). He was essentially a fluffy retriever that didn't shed, which is said to be helpful for those with allergies. Everything was great, until we brought the dog home and my daughter who has OCD realised that there was a dog that was full of germs in her house and as each day passed, the dog got bigger... A lot bigger. The little girl who had begged and pleaded for a dog suddenly hated this new puppy and begged and pleaded for us to return him. We did a lot of work on how having a dog can actually boost your immune system and how to keep herself clean without going overboard and it took a year and a half but now her and the dog are firm friends.

My son, the one that didn't want a dog now has his own therapy dog that he can't do without. When he has a meltdown, the dog is the first one there and can calm him down and bring him back to his normal state within minutes. When he feels lonely the dog is there for him, always ready to catch a ball or play hide and seek and they have an amazing bond.

The popularity of horses as therapy animals continues to rise, alongside that of dogs. As well as increasing a child's mental wellbeing, horses can also help with improving motor skills. There are many organizations that can provide equine and canine therapy for those with autism which may be a preferred option to the commitment of buying a pet.

Bach Remedy Rescue – If your child suffers from anxiety, Bach Remedy Rescue may help. There are various forms you can buy, from pastilles to pillow sprays and most supermarkets and high street chemists stock them. Remedy Rescue is made from flower extracts and is gentle enough to be given to very young children. When my son was about six years of age he learned about Van Gogh at school and all of a sudden in the middle of a trip to the Isle of Wight he got really distraught, he was certain his ears were falling off. I went to the closest pharmacy and asked what they recommended and that was how I found Remedy Rescue. We called them his 'calm down sweets' and when we returned home his school even let us give some to his teacher, so that he could access them if needed during the day. He stopped using them after a while, but we kept a pack in the house in case of emergencies for a couple of years afterwards.

Keeping the noise down – When we tell the children to stop shouting, they get really irritated. We spend a lot of time in our house saying, "be quiet, I'm right next to you." The problem is that some children with autism are unable to appropriately modulate their volume. We have spent years helping the children to be aware of how loud they are talking, but especially when they are excited, it is just beyond their control. It can be extremely awkward when your child starts talking about someone else in the room, thinking that they are whispering but are talking so loudly that everyone else can hear every word.

Online there are useful volume modulators that you can make to let children know when they are speaking at an appropriate level however, be careful how you address it with your children as there is the danger that they could feel self-conscious about it and stop speaking altogether or going too far the other way and whisper all of the time.

Temperature – I don't know about you, but I think I gave birth to Baby Bear and Goldilocks because they both like their food to be just right. My son was told he couldn't have school dinners and had to bring packed lunches after an incident. Basically, his dinner was too hot for him, he was so busy talking that he missed the 'perfect window' and when he tried to eat it, the food was too cold. The dinner ladies wouldn't let him leave until he'd eaten and so he got angry and stormed out. Packed lunches were just as much of a minefield, he wouldn't eat or drink anything unless it was chilled properly. Every day I send them off with a cool block in his lunch bag that has been frozen overnight, in a bid to keep their food and drink as cool as possible.

Each time there's a class trip, the letter always states disposable items only, but I've always negotiated that he can take his lunch bag, because that cool block is vital. You can buy them from supermarkets, for a small cost, but they are effective if your child needs their food or drink to be chilled. Talk to the class teacher to see what can be done, if this is an issue for your child whenever there's a school trip.

Laces – Because of his lack of fine motor skills, my son was never able to tie his own laces. It was never a problem, we simply bought Velcro shoes. Years passed without us realising and suddenly he was in an adult size six and needed lace up rugby boots and finding Velcro shoes became a challenge. His first day at Secondary school was hideous for him because he'd decided to wear shoes with laces and spent the whole day fiddling with them when the shoes came loose.

Luckily, there are different variations of self-tying laces available online and I was able to order some for next day delivery and it means that my son can wear any shoes now. Self-tying laces come in so many different colours and now he's empowered and not restricted.

Theatre clubs – Every time I spoke to the Paediatrician about my son's shyness she kept telling me I should enrol him in a drama group. The very idea of this sent my son into a meltdown, so it was not an avenue we went down. I did propose the idea to my daughter and got pretty much the same response that my son had given. However, for some children this could be a good way of boosting self-esteem, interacting with peers, promoting resilience and independence.

Don't use the word naughty – If you use the word 'naughty' it gives the child a label to live down to. If that's what they're going to be named as, then why would they try to be anything else? You can say that a specific behaviour was naughty, as in 'biting your sister was naughty,' but not simply to say the child is naughty.

Where possible, always state the positives, I know this isn't always easy but in the long run the effects on your child will be far more positive in terms of their mental health.

Lava Lamps – Classic lava lamps, the homemade variety made from YouTube videos and other similar objects have calming effects on children with autism. The slow movement, the colours, the constant change and the texture can be a distraction and can help the child to regulate their emotional state.

Reflection and containment – We are only human, no one is perfect one hundred percent of the time (with the possible exception of Zac Efron.) The only way we can improve, is to reflect on where we went wrong if an incident ended negatively and then understand how not to repeat the pattern. This needs to be done when you have time to think properly and to consider who said what, how it was said etc in detail. Children respond well to boundaries and when everything else seems to be out of their control, knowing that their parents can handle the bad times and still love them unconditionally can have a hugely powerful and calming effect on a child.

Gaming – My children were born to game, it's all they've ever wanted to do. I often have to sit and bite my tongue when I hear other parents or professionals preaching about the evils of gaming. I've had conversations with them about people online not always being who they say they are and they don't ever talk to people that they haven't already met in the real world and I'm as comfortable as I can be that they are safe online. As long as they have done their homework I positively encourage them to have their downtime and they are straight on one of their many consoles.

My two have never have been the outdoors type and I don't think they ever will be. They made me buy two pop-up-tents recently, so they could camp out in the living room, because they don't like the outdoors and having to deal with other people. At the weekend we have one day out, but we also have a day where the kids can relax and do what they want. Sometimes they watch Netflix, or read a book, but generally it's gaming.

It hasn't been all plain sailing, when the Wi-Fi goes down, all hell breaks loose. Similarly, getting them off of their game to eat their food or have a conversation can cause upset, but there is one area where all these issues are worth it and that is socialising. We live in a different city to where my children attend school. Our school run is a twenty-five-mile round trip. If you add the distance, to the social isolation of being an Aspie in a mainstream school, this always meant that whilst other parents were boasting on social media about meeting up in the park for play dates, my children were on their own and didn't see a classmate until school began again. That all changed when my son joined secondary school and met a group of friends who all had Xboxes. All of a sudden, he was connected to his friends when they weren't at school. I am the opposite of most parents, because I encourage him to go on the Xbox and get worried if he hasn't been on there talking to his friends, concerned that there might have been some sort of falling out. The best sound in the world to me is him chattering away into a headset. I often pop into his room to double check who he's playing against, to ensure it's always just the boys from his friendship group at school. This way of socialising particularly works for him, because he can leave the game whenever he wants, which is not as overwhelming as having a group of friends physically in his room. It has dramatically improved his self-esteem and his emotional regulation at school and has been nothing but positive, so being online is not always a negative, as long as the child can understand about staying safe.

Hitting – Physical violence is one of the most anti-social of behaviours and is going to be the least tolerated in a school environment. If you can't verbalise your anger and frustration, it is also the most natural explosion of emotion. If your child is hurting others and possibly yourself it is happening as a reaction to extreme anxiety. It may be difficult but remain calm and don't retaliate in kind. Let the child know in a firm way that it is unacceptable and if appropriate give them time to calm down safely. Physical sports that allow the child to get all of their aggression out, like boxing may be worth trying as they can be very effective in anger reduction.

Around the age of five, boys get a testosterone boost and my son became extremely aggressive. I knew I had to nip his outbursts in the bud, because that level of aggression at an older age was terrifying. I'm forty-two years of age and I am still scared of my parents, yet at five my son didn't have that same respect or recognise that there is a line you don't cross. In my desperation I thought back to what my parents did to keep me in line and decided to give it a try. I said to my son "if you can't accept our rules, you're going to have to live in a children's home. Do you want to go to a children's home?" Without even blinking and with genuine sincerity and perhaps a slight touch of defiance, he said "I don't know, what's the food like?" It was time for Plan B...

The next day on the way back from school he was becoming increasingly aggressive, so I pulled into the car park of the local police station and told him to get out. He went from angry to terrified in the blink of an eye. I told him that aggressive boys end up in jail, so I was going to drop him off and they could deal with him. He begged me to take him home and promised he would be good. After that, whenever he was starting to get violent I would grab my keys and tell him to get in the car and instantly he would calm down. Even now if we see police, he says "keep walking, keep walking." I recognise it was extreme, but so was his behaviour and I had his baby sister's safety to consider and it worked. I wouldn't advise leaving a child alone as a shock tactic, as this is too extreme, but sometimes thinking creatively can solve certain issues.

Processing time – Children on the spectrum can have difficulty in interpreting the signals from their body and this takes more time than for TD peers. Most people who haven't got autism can hear what someone has said to them and then respond in an appropriate amount of time, those with autism can't. In my experience schools are the worst offenders for forgetting this. To be fair school time is limited and they have at least another twenty-five children in a mainstream school to deal with at any one time, but it doesn't change the fact that children with autism need time to react. I've seen teachers either dismiss what a child has to say because they can't get it out fast enough or they've shouted in a child's face "answer me!" as if that child was deliberately taking their time to answer.

Children with autism hear what is said and then need time to absorb what they have heard, work out how they feel about it and how they want to respond. This takes time when you're on the spectrum, but it doesn't mean that they haven't got opinions or a valid point of view, you just need to be mindful that they need extra processing time to get their words out.

In the past I have been very guilty of trying to help my son come to a decision, by offering different choices. He shouted at me "you're not helping. You're just confusing me." Decisions have to be made internally and outside influences may mean that the decision-making process takes longer, so be patient, it will be worth it.

Girls on the spectrum

The gap is steadily closing between the number of females being diagnosed with autism, versus the number of males. Most females aren't diagnosed until they are in their forties, they are more likely to have been diagnosed with social anxiety first rather than autism and have spent decades trying to cope without a diagnosis or understanding. Most of the early research around autism was centred around boys and professionals are only just beginning to better identify the specific autistic traits of girls, which are different to those of boys.

In a school situation, boys generally externalise their anxiety and anger in disruptive behaviour and are far more likely to be referred to professionals for assessment because they are causing the teacher problems. The 'shy,' 'anxious' girl sat quietly in the back, sometimes crying to herself isn't causing disruption to the teacher and the rest of the class and will generally be overlooked.

I don't like to use stereotypes, but commonly a boy who doesn't understand what he's being asked to do, will react angrily. The difference in girls is that they internalise their anxiety and are more socially adept at getting their needs met. Girls are watchers and imitators, and this is how they slip under the radar so often. They will quietly ask one of their classmates what the task is and then do their best to get on with it, their aim is to not draw attention to themselves.

This ability to hide in plain sight does however get more difficult as they get older. The world of adolescent girls is a social one and suddenly the gap widens between girls on the autistic spectrum and their TD peers.

Girls have more socially acceptable obsessions, such as animals and celebrities. They can however get very intense in their friendships and will get jealous if their 'best friend' has other friends.

Girls often find it easier to escape into books, fantasy worlds, their own imagination and roleplay, which can give them more confidence, they can behind a character rather than being themselves. My daughter spent a whole three weeks only responding to then name Gromit and walked around on all fours, I drew the line at putting her food in a bowl.

One of the differences between girls and boys is that boys are mainly obsessed with objects, whereas girls are generally more obsessed with people or animals. Girls typically have a more sophisticated vocabulary, and this can obscure their communication difficulties. They give the impression that they are more emotionally aware than they actually are.

Pathological Demand Avoidance

Pathological Demand Avoidance (PDA) is still a controversial topic of debate. As a condition it is not recognised by all professionals, however it is acknowledged by the National Autistic Society. PDA was first identified by Professor Elizabeth Newson in the early eighties and is typified by a need to control, born out of anxiety. It is not a stand-alone condition and is only found in those with an autistic diagnosis.

Although PDA comes under the autism umbrella, children with this condition have a specific set of traits that do not completely fit into the ASD or Asperger's diagnostic criteria. Children with PDA were usually passive, good natured babies and very easy going for the first twelve months and without speech delay. The main difference is that these children are more socially adept than others with autism, as they seek subtle ways to avoid what is being asked of them and can be quite chatty.

Generally, you don't give a child with autism choices as this confuses them and can make them feel overwhelmed, but PDA is different in this respect. Anxiety is raised when the child feels a lack of control and so for instance when I realised that going to nursery was a trigger for my daughter, I would say "OK, when you go to nursery today, do you want to wear the red t-shirt or the green t-shirt." This took away the anxiety about going to nursery. Attending was non-negotiable (she only went two afternoons per week for socialisation), but I had made her feel as though she had a say by choosing what she wanted to wear.

When you ask a child with PDA to do something, such as pick up a pencil, they will suddenly switch the subject to try and deflect you from thinking about what you asked them to do. This can be done so subtly that you may not even be aware that you're being manipulated by a master. If changing the subject doesn't work, then they will often come up with far-fetched reasons as to why they can't comply but will be very sincere. Their response will be something like 'well I'd love to pick up the pencil but I'm afraid I can't because my leg just fell off.' At other times, they will try and wear you down by trying to negotiate and If they feel threatened, then they may even become aggressive.

When a child with autism has a meltdown, it can take them a long time to calm down after, however for a child with PDA their mood can change, as swiftly as pressing a light switch. Children with PDA can be extremely charming, and peers may be drawn to them, but often their dominating nature can alienate peers just as easily.

Professionals are more comfortable diagnosing Oppositional Defiant Disorder (ODD) which is more in keeping with the aggressive side of PDA and is a recognised condition, unlike PDA and so diagnosis is difficult to come by. The name PDA is well known amongst parents of children with autism and the conversation is continuing as to whether this should be a professionally recognised condition.

School days

One of the environments that can cause the most anxiety for a child on the autistic spectrum is school. Due to inclusion reforms in schools there are ever more children with autism entering mainstream school. Statistics state that seventeen percent of children with autism have been suspended from school. Forty eight percent of these had been suspended a minimum of three times and four percent had been expelled from at least one school. Anyone who works in a school would most likely believe the statistic that three children in every classroom has a mental health problem is something of an underestimation.

Although inclusion is a positive strategy it can still have some negative impacts on the child, when they are placed in large sized classes and with members of staff who may not know how or be able to help children with special needs. I hear from other parents of diagnosed children how drained they are with the constant encounters against schools. It is unfortunate that it is always seen as a battle; which then turns the school into an enemy and an opposing force, when they are the ones who have the care of your children on a daily basis. Sadly, if you spend any time talking to parents, the majority of them will use the word 'battle.'

An understanding Headteacher, a SENDCo who has the autonomy to make decisions and follow them through and a class teacher that believes every child deserves as education shouldn't be difficult to find, yet sadly this is often not the experience that parents are faced with. This is why there are a large number of children with autism who are home schooled.

Over the years I have found the responsibility of being a 'warrior' defending my children both empowering and exhausting. No matter how frustrated I got, the fact remained the same that if I didn't do it, who else was going to stand up for them. As a parent I have experienced both good and bad schools, thankfully both my children are now in schools where they are happy and understood; but there were so many years before when they weren't.

I have also worked in schools where the whole school ethos was inclusion and celebrating differences, all the way through to ones where staff members happily made derogatory comments about children with special needs and SENDCOs were not allowed to make changes that would help improve the lives of the children. In fact, I have seen a culture of deliberately triggering meltdowns and negative behaviour.

At one parent teacher meeting, I asked one of my son's teachers if they could make a small allowance over something and the reply was "if I do that for him, I'd have to do that for the normal children." I don't think I had ever been so angry in my whole life, to make matters worse my son was sat next to me when the teacher referred to him as not being normal. I won't recount what I said to the teacher as it would fill the rest of this book and make it X rated, but rest assured I put him in his place; detailed his ignorance and made a formal complaint which was effectively dealt with by the school and my son no longer has this person as a teacher. I can't believe that these attitudes still exist in this day and age.

One of the most painful consequences of school that parents of autistic children will identify with is the handing out of party invitations. I have mothers of TD children telling me "oh you can't take it personally," when myself and my child have found ourselves standing in the playground surrounded by a smug kid handing out little envelopes and the lucky few running to their parents waving the invitations around as if they were golden tickets. It is utterly destroying, when you see the look on your child's face, the slump of the shoulders and the words "why haven't I been invited?"

Equally it was terrifying when they did get an invite, because it invariably meant that I would need to stay in case they got overwhelmed and would be able to see up close and personal, the differences in my children and the rest of their classmates. Every game that resulted in a prize at the end resulted in a meltdown because my child couldn't complete the tasks in the same way as their peers and couldn't understand why they never won.

At a very young age, children are suddenly thrust into a world full of strangers where they are expected to obey abstract rules that they might not fully understand and find themselves getting shouted at by strange adults for unintentionally doing something wrong. They are not even permitted to go to the toilet or eat or drink when they want to, without a stranger's permission. When I worked with children who had just entered full-time schooling I was constantly being asked "is it home time now?" when it wasn't even ten o'clock in the morning. When you're little, the school day is a long, bewildering day. It may also be the first time that the child is faced with other children who have their own special needs and conflict happens at this age quite frequently.

No matter how accommodating a mainstream school is, the teacher still has over thirty children whose needs and behaviours have to be taken into account and manage and with the best will in the world they can forget a child's triggers or spot signs of a meltdown when they have a set timetable to follow.

School refusal – The term 'school refusal' sounds as though the child is simply deciding that they don't want to go to school. There are lots of children without special needs, who given the choice would probably choose not to go to school and stay at home, but this isn't about a child's whim. School refusal is often accompanied by vomiting, stomach aches, crying, running away, meltdowns, insomnia and sleep walking. Their anxiety is so high that they are experiencing extremely elevated panic levels and are terrified. There is usually a trigger that causes the school refusal, such as bullying and so a conversation with the school needs to be had as soon as possible in order to identify what has caused the anxiety.

Normally the school and parents along with any necessary external agencies can work together to find the cause of the anxiety and resolve it. Some approaches can include a staged reintegration to school where the child returns for half day sessions before returning to full time schooling.

Split Personality in school and at home – One of the most difficult and challenging things I've found with being a parent of two children with Asperger's Syndrome is trying to impress on the school, the effect that some of their decisions were having on my children, particularly my daughter. I often thought that they had written me off as a neurotic mother who just made everything up in order to get attention or to satisfy my own anxieties. In my son's case it wasn't too difficult, he externalised his anxiety and anger and so they were plain to see. There was a definite correlation between the class teacher announcing something that upset him and my son reacting negatively. My daughter however was another matter. My little girl wouldn't dream of debating anything with her teacher and would do anything to avoid drawing attention to herself. So, if a planned school event or one of her peers had upset her during the day she would show absolutely no outward emotion until she got home and then she let all of her feelings out. I would be the one who would see the result of her anxieties, deal with the extra insomnia, the sleepwalking, the stomach aches, the anger, the tears and the outright refusals to go to school. I would promise her that I would go into school and sort it out the next day, so she would go into class all happy and the class teacher was none the wiser. Luckily, the school SENDCo understood that this was quite common and just because she was displaying no signs of anxiety at school, it didn't mean that they weren't there.

The impact of holding your emotions and behaviour in total control for a whole day, can cause the child's emotions to explode at home. I had one friend whose child walked out of school and smashed one of the windows of her car, by kicking it in the middle of a meltdown, he had been waiting all day to release his frustration.

If this is the case with your child, then make sure you talk to the school and let them know what goes on after the school bell goes at the end of the day. What is happening at home, as a direct result of the school day is going to eventually impact on the classroom at some point, so to help themselves and help your child they need to be aware. If you feel like you are constantly at the school asking to see the class teacher or the SENDCo, you could ask about a home/school book, this will enable you to write down any concerns in it and the teacher can look at it without your child, or more importantly other children or parents overhearing.

Specialist Schools – I believe in inclusion because children with special needs are a part of society and shouldn't be hidden away in schools by themselves. However, for some children mainstream school cannot meet their needs. I have seen children whose parents were adamant that they should remain in mainstream school, getting farther and farther behind and increasingly distressed and isolated. I have also seen children leave mainstream school for a specialist school where they have suddenly been accepted and allowed to be themselves, in a smaller class with knowledgeable staff, these children have been able to positively thrive. Every child is different, and one size doesn't fit all.

A majority of parents have no knowledge of what a specialist school is like. If you think your child may benefit from attending one, then ask for a tour of an appropriate local school and you will probably be amazed at their facilities and how they are such positive environments. There are generally waiting lists for specialist schools and you would need your child's current school to hold an annual review as a letter from an Ed Psych stating that the child's needs cannot be met at their mainstream school will be needed, before you can apply for a place.

Individual Education Plan (IEP) – You may be asked to sign an IEP for your child, which the school will have prepared. The IEP is a list of targets and explains who is responsible for helping the child to achieve them and by what date. IEPs are reviewed in order to plan the next one, once the deadline of the previous IEP had been reached; this allows the effectiveness of the support that the child has received to be assessed and improved.

SEND Code of Practice – The Special Educational Needs and Disability Code of Practice is statutory guidance that local authorities, health bodies, schools and colleges etc in England are required to follow, when caring for children with special educational needs. It is a comprehensive piece of guidance that protects those with special needs and disabilities and is useful for parents to find out what their child is entitled to and can be used in meetings to make your point, if you feel there is something that is lacking from your child's educational provision. The Code of Practice is available online for free.

Equality Act 2010 – The Equality Act draws together previous regulation into one act. The act sets out the responsibilities of various bodies such as workplaces and schools in terms of discrimination and harassment. It is a long piece of legislation but can be viewed online for free and is an invaluable source of advice, if you believe your child is being discriminated against.

Inclusion – The debate surrounding inclusion in mainstream school still continues to rage. If you have a child with special educational needs, then you are more likely to agree that inclusion is positive. However, if your child is scared to go to school because there is a classmate who is physically violent and harming their peers, you may not be so happy about it. I've seen both sides but, on the whole, I believe it is positive. However there needs to be sufficient support in place, to enable the child to access all parts of the curriculum. Schools cannot discriminate due to disabilities and special educational needs, so if your child is not being sufficiently included, challenge this decision.

Exclusion – Children in England don't have to be in full-time education until the start of term following their fifth birthday. Because of this, my son was excluded from afternoon school throughout the whole year in Reception. Each day we had to collect him at lunchtime, whilst all of his friends were happily having school dinners and running around the playground. Whenever he had done something that was considered to be disruptive etc, we would get a phone call and had to immediately collect him, and he was excluded until the following school day.

I had almost forgotten about this until last week when I began talking to a family of a child with autism who was aged seven. Their little boy was being excluded by the school for the same reason as my son. The parents had been told that their child was only able to attend school during the mornings as the school did not have the funds to employ a full-time teaching assistant to support him. The difference with this family, was that their child was within the age limit of compulsory school age and must receive a full-time education. It saddens me that children are still being failed in this way and this particular family lived on the east coast, the opposite end of the country to us so it's not even a local issue. A parent may not realise their rights and believe that the school is acting within the law at all times.

There are two kinds of expulsion that can be applied to a child. A fixed period suspension and a permanent exclusion. When a child is suspended, the school is only able to exclude them for a maximum of forty-five days in a school year even if they have recently changed schools. The school must set work and mark it for the first five days. If the child is suspended for more than five days the school must arrange full-time educational provision for the child, which may not necessarily take place at the school but could be in a referral unit. If the school makes alternative arrangements, it is your responsibility to make sure your child attends and receives their education. If your child has been permanently excluded, then your local authority must find full-time educational provision for them from the sixth day of the exclusion. If in doubt, the National Autistic Society and Citizens Advice helplines are excellent places to find out what your rights are and how to appeal a school's decision.

Private Workspace – One Saturday morning I received a phone call from a friend, whose daughter was in my son's Year One class. She'd wanted to tell me that her daughter was upset because my son had been forced to sit alone facing a wall and she wanted to know whether I was aware that this was happening… I wasn't.

I felt like I'd been punched in the stomach and hadn't seen the fist coming at me. If her daughter was so upset, then how did my son feel? Why hadn't he told me? So many questions went through my mind in those few seconds. I tried to sound calm and thanked her for letting me know and hung up as quickly as possible. I asked my little boy whether he sat on his own at school and he said, "yes I distract everyone, so I sit facing the wall on a table on my own."

I spent the rest of the weekend getting angrier and angrier and by Monday morning I was ready and waiting for the teacher before school. Trying to remain calm after two days of getting myself wound up and ready to do battle, I had to restrain myself. I asked her what she thought she was doing, putting my son into isolation in front of the rest of the class. I told her how I'd been called by the Mum of an upset classmate and demanded that she sit him on a table with the other children. The teacher looked really apologetic and explained that it had been my son's suggestion to sit by himself. He thought that he was less likely to get into trouble if he wasn't constantly talking to other children and found it easier to concentrate... At no point throughout the weekend when we had been talking about it, had my son mentioned that it had been his idea and it was actually working out well for him. I was mortified.

In the years that have followed, I've found out that sitting a child with autism by themselves for certain parts of the day (not all day) was endorsed by the school's autism outreach service and is relatively common practice. Since I started working in a school I have seen the benefits to children with special needs in being able to focus without distractions or temptations; however, it should not be permanent and become the seat that the child always stays at throughout the school day. If the child only sits at a table by themselves there is the danger it will be seen as a permanent time out and the other children may think they are naughty. Inclusion back into a group with peers should be the main goal.

Walking long distances – Due to the lack of motor skills in some children on the spectrum, they may also lack muscle tone and can tire out very easily, as well as seeming clumsy and likely to trip up frequently. If your child has difficulties in walking long distances then before they embark on any school trips, speak to the school and find out how much walking is planned and whether it is will be on flat ground as opposed to mountain trekking and ask them to find a way of making it as accessible to your child as possible.

Visual Timetable – Most mainstream schools, especially reception classes are aware of the benefits and importance of visual timetables; they are a useful visual tool for all children and help to minimise anxiety. If you think a visual timetable could be useful for your child, talk to their class teacher or the SENDCo about making or buying one in. It can be introduced as something for the whole class to use and not something that will single your child out amongst their peers as needing extra help, if that is something they might be nervous about.

Targets – Your child will probably be set various targets, especially if they have an IEP or EHCP. These targets will normally be set by the school

however you and your child may be asked for input. When setting targets make sure that they are 'SMART.'
Specific
Measurable
Achievable
Relevant
Time-bound.

Policies – Every school must have their policies visible on their website. Their SEND policy will be a good place to start if you think that the school is not meeting its responsibilities.

Choices of Secondary School – If your child is in primary school and has an EHCP, choosing a Secondary School will be different process than for children without one. During your child's annual review in Year Five, you will be asked your preference for secondary school. Children with EHCPs are high on the allocated spaces priority list and this is a great benefit in a time of possible anxiety. If the school you have chosen has a good understanding of SEN children, they will arrange transition sessions for your child before they start school and will want to know as much as possible about your child in order to support them.

When touring a prospective school, take your child with you if possible as they may think of questions or raise anxieties that you may not have thought of. As much exposure as possible to the school environment will help the transition. You could ask the school if it would be possible for you to take photos so that over the summer holidays your child can familiarise themselves with their new school.

Year Seven Teething Troubles – For children with autism, starting secondary school can be a difficult transition to make. For seven years they have been at a school where they usually have one teacher for the whole day and if they have had teaching assistant support, that will usually be provided by the same person. If your child has had a bad night or isn't feeling well, you can always pop in and tell the teacher before the start of the school day and ask them to keep an eye on them. You can't do this in secondary school.

Suddenly, they have at least five different teachers in one day and any one to one support may be with a different person for each subject. They move from one class to another along with hundreds of other children and are responsible for packing up and carrying their own belongings.

After seven years, they are suddenly confronted with strange new pupils, who may not be as accepting of them. In most cases every day will differ, and timetables can alternate between week one and week two. It is no wonder that children with autism can find secondary school difficult to adjust to.

Transition sessions can help, as well as a good SEN team in the school. Generally, it does get better by the time they begin year eight but keep talking to the school to try and avoid any potential issues. My son's meltdown trigger was PE and so his school allowed him to go to the SEN building and do homework, whilst slowly reintroducing him back into PE lessons almost a year later. I know several autistic children who don't attend language lessons for the same reason. Secondary Schools can be more flexible and accommodating than primary schools, so it is worth talking to them about what they can do for your child.

Bullying – If your child becomes withdrawn and anxious about going to school at any age then it's possible that they may be being bullied. If you are concerned that your child's personality has changed, then speak to them about what's been going on and/or the school.

When your child is in secondary school then pay particular attention to them becoming withdrawn. Social friendships are far more important in adolescence and the older the children, the more serious the bullying can be. The only reason I knew something was going on, was because my normally chatty boy suddenly became sullen and silent in the car after school.

If your child is being bullied and needs to talk about it to someone, there are various local charities such as Off the Record, which the school or your GP will be able to give you details for. If your child is finding it particularly difficult, you could also request a CAMHS referral.

Detentions and Consequences - Don't let schools carry punishment on to the next day. If your child needs to have a detention and miss out on playtime then it needs to be carried out on the same day and not carried over to the next. If a detention takes place the following day then those feelings of anger and frustration are going to resurface and most likely the child will end up with another detention. The response from most teaching staff is 'well I'm busy at breaktime and so it has to be tomorrow.' I've had to politely point out to them that it's not my child's problem. If they can't offer a detention that day, then they need to take away a good behaviour point or make some time to talk about what went wrong and what the expectations are instead.

As a teacher, if you have a child in your class who is struggling to cope in the classroom and is having a particularly bad day; the worst thing you could do is to stop that child from running around and letting off steam. To keep a child who struggles with sitting for long periods at a time, to remain sitting when they can hear and possibly see other children running around, is cruel and counter-productive. The child will be more full of energy in following lessons, less likely to focus and co-operate and more likely to be more volatile and aggressive; schools need to adapt how they carry out consequences for unwanted behaviour.

Assessments – My favourite quote is one that I think really sums up a common experience of children with autism in a mainstream school environment. The quote is "Everyone is a genius. But if you judge a fish by its ability to climb a tree, it will live its whole life being that it is stupid."

The way children are assessed and taught in mainstream schools, is often not the most beneficial environment for children on the spectrum and as parents we understand that if you use a one size fits all approach, some children are going to be left out and aren't able to flourish.

There are minimal tweaks that can often be made that are sometimes overlooked because the school has an itinerary they need to follow and lots of other children to consider, so it can always be useful to make suggestions. If you can pre-empt a meltdown then everyone is going to benefit.

Not all children want to be the centre of attention and don't want to be up on the stage during assemblies, so in the past at school we have given children a camcorder on a tripod for them to film the assembly for parents that couldn't get there, which made the children feel really important and involved.

Another ordeal for some, can be sports day. It can be overwhelming to stand in front of lots of shouting and cheering people, the noise is completely deafening. It can be humiliating too, for children that cannot keep up. For some it can be a lesson in resilience and even though they are last they still get a massive cheer from the spectators. My son however, burst into tears and lay face down in the middle of the track crying his eyes out. For children who want to be involved but don't want to race, we have given them a stopwatch and a clipboard with paper and pencil to record the results, whilst other children have been the 'official photographer'.

None of the little tweaks we made cost money, but it made a huge difference to the children's
self-esteem;' allowing them to be included on their own terms.

The Thrive Approach – The Thrive Approach is a programme that schools can subscribe to, which gives strategies and assessments for children with emotional or behavioural issues. It is a great programme which tailors interventions to specific children and can produce excellent results. If your child is having difficulties at school, ask the class teacher or SENDCo if the school uses The Thrive Approach and whether it would be appropriate for your child.

Filling in paperwork – In order for your child to access the help they need, it is likely that you are going to be asked to fill in some paperwork. Evidence is needed to support applications for things such as an EHCP or Disability Living Allowance. The first time you have to do this can be awful. I felt as though I were betraying my son, by listing all of his faults and using them against him. Until this point I had only ever focused on positives and I was worried that at some point in the future he would read my comments and be deeply upset. Worse still was when I had to attend the meetings concerning the paperwork and the school were listing all these negatives and there were absolutely no positives. It took a long time for me to realise that the school had to focus on the negatives in order to claim financial support. They have to consider his worse days and as a parent that was really difficult to hear. You can leave those sorts of meetings feeling quite low, tearful, shaken, totally without help and completely alone. Try to think of these meetings in the context of getting help and try and remain calm, it will hopefully benefit your child at the end of the process.

Becoming more independent – As a parent of a child with special needs, you become so used to helping them so that they don't have a meltdown that all of a sudden, they're teenagers and you're still doing everything.
When my son was ten, a lot of the local children started calling for one another after school and hanging out around the area until later in the evening. I asked him "would you like to go and call for one of your friends one night?" and his answer was one of pure outrage as if I'd gone completely mad. He said "good God woman, have you never heard of Paedophiles? I won't be calling for anyone until I'm at least eighteen" and

walked off shaking his head. He's thirteen now and so far, he hasn't changed his mind about calling for friends or my abilities as a mother.

It may take a little longer for children on the spectrum to meet certain milestones, but don't give up hope that they won't. After years of trying, one day they will just do something that you never thought possible. It is important to encourage independence, it will help their resilience. However, try to ensure that any leaps they make are safe and achievable, don't set them up to fail.

Home Schooling – Common problems with mainstream schools, such as lack of understanding, large class sizes and bullying have led parents to home school their children. Most children do very well being home schooled, and it can be a great relief to both the child and their parents to be in a safe environment. There are no set rules of what must be taught and when and some parents use tutors to help with certain subjects. One of the key concerns about home schooling is socialisation, however some of those who choose to home educate believe that children should socialise with people of all ages and not just children. There are strong links amongst the home schooling community and children can meet up with peers who are also educated at home, so that they still have the opportunity to socialise with their peers. Education Otherwise, is one of the organisations that gives information about home schooling and there is a wealth of information online if this is something you are considering.

Other parents – They don't mean it, but parents of children without autism or special needs in general just don't have the same fears, battles and anxieties that we do. It can be difficult to stand in a group talking about your children going on a school trip for example and the other parents have no concerns about their children going off on a residential school trip and for you it's the worst thing you've had to deal with so far. It can feel really demoralising to be told "don't worry, they'll be fine" as if you're just being neurotic and you haven't got a child that may need medication, behavioural problems or separation anxiety. Whenever my son had residential trips, we had to book hotels in the vicinity so that we could pick him up at bedtime and drop him back straight after breakfast so that he could still participate at his own level. If I had sent him off I know full well I would have had a phone call in the middle of the night telling me to come and pick him up and he would have missed out on the remainder of the trip.

The only thing worse than unintentional patronisation is when parents don't talk to you at all and you're just as isolated in the playground as your child is. Sometimes this happens, because the other children have gone home and told their parents all about the 'naughty' child that hurt them and so you are shunned; or I've known parents who have thought that their child's reputation was well known and have stood in a corner of the playground with their arms defensively folded and then it's a self-fulfilling prophecy when they are left standing by themselves. I've known other parents who sit in their car until the very last minute so that they don't need to speak to anyone in the playground.

If you feel like this then try not to worry, it's probably not as bad as you think and you're definitely not alone. You could find out if the school holds coffee mornings for SEN parents and if they don't, why not suggest it to the SENDCo? Being around others going through the same issues can be helpful and are definitely worth seeking.

Bad Parenting – I've lost count of the number of times I've heard parents tell me that they've been judged by strangers who feel it's fine to make comments, when out in public with their child. Others have been very upset at being sent on a parenting course before their children were diagnosed and felt that the professionals were blaming their child's condition on them. Once I went to a local parent and carers group and sat next to a mum who spent most of the morning explaining to me why she didn't like parents of autistic children. She said that we feel it's okay for our children to act how they want, because of their autism. After the initial shock wore off, I defiantly defended autism parents, but I honestly don't think I changed her mind one bit. It is unfair and ignorant to both the parents and to the children to lay blame or judgement on them. Children with autism have a neurological disability and their parents are doing the best job that they can. There is a fine line between doing nothing and allowing for the autism. Children on the spectrum have deficiencies in their social interactions and it is our job to explain the rules and navigate them through social situations, but at the same time they have a disability and can't be punished in the same way as TD peers.

Sensory overload – The world is full of overwhelming sights and sounds for a child on the autistic spectrum. The inability to process so much information in one go, can cause the whole system to shut-down. In order to keep them as calm as possible, try to reduce distractions and the possibility of sensory overload. Your child may display signs that they are experiencing sensory overload by displaying repetitive regulation behaviour, such as hand flapping.

Where possible try to keep decoration to a minimum and have a room that is quite plain where a child can calm down. If this is not practical, it may help for a child to wear dark sunglasses to reduce their level of visual stimulation. Touch, smells and too much noise can also cause overload, so be aware of this and try to reduce them as much as possible. I carried around sunglasses and ear defenders for years in my handbag because I could never predict when they would be needed. To ensure my daughter wouldn't feel so self-conscious about wearing ear defenders, I bought several bags of pink Swarovski crystals and glued them on, which she loved.

Benefits and Resources

Proof of Disability Card – In the local authority that I live in, they have a child's disability register and when your child is voluntarily added to the register they are sent a pink card with the council's logo and the name of the child stating that they are on the disability register. We are then able to use this card as proof of disability to get concessions whenever we go anywhere that charges for entry. Local authorities differ, and some may have a similar car system, or you can apply online for various other types of Proof of Disability cards, such as the Access card for entertainment venues. An online search can provide a variety of options, depending on what your needs and hobbies are, there may be one that is more appropriate than another.

Cinema Discounts – If your child is eight years of age or over and receives Disability Living Allowance or Personal Independence Payment and they like to visit cinemas, then you may be eligible for a Cinema Exhibitors' Association (CEA) card. For a small fee you can claim a card from the CEA website, which will need to be renewed every twelve months. The idea is that you only pay for your child's ticket as you get one free adult carer's ticket. Don't forget that many cinemas now hold autism friendly showings, which have low lighting but aren't completely dark and children are welcome to move around and make noise if they need to in a safe and understanding place with children who have the same needs.

Theme Parks – When visiting theme parks such as Legoland or a Disney park and your child has a problem with queuing, then you need a letter from a professional such as a Paediatrician which specifically states their diagnosis and their inability to wait in a queue. When you get to the park, if you go to Guest Services they will give you a pass that enables you to book one ride at a time through a virtual queuing system, so that your child doesn't have to physically wait in a queue. For some families, mine included, it is the only way that theme parks can be visited and makes the day so much easier. Be aware that simply having a letter that states a diagnosis is not enough, it must say that the child has a problem waiting in line. Each park may have slightly different terms and conditions which change over time, so check their websites before you visit.

Disability Living Allowance/Personal Independence Payment - You don't have to wait for a diagnosis of a condition to claim Disability Living Allowance (DLA) or the new Personal Independence Payment (PIP), the assessment is based on need not diagnosis. If your child struggles with mobility or has intense consistent care needs, then you can contact the helpline or apply online. Local support groups can usually offer help filling in the form if needed.

Tax Credits/Universal Credit – There are two types of tax credits, Child Tax Credit and Working Tax Credit. If your child is under sixteen, or under twenty and in full time education or training, then you may be eligible to apply for Child Tax Credit. If you work at least sixteen hours per week then you may also be able to apply for Working Tax Credit or Universal Credit. The Government website has a tax credits calculator you can complete to check what you may be eligible for and you can apply directly online.

Carer's Allowance – For anyone whose child receives DLA or PIP, you may be able to claim Carer's Allowance if you earn no more than one hundred and twenty pounds per week after tax and are not a full-time student. You can apply over the phone and if you do receive a reward you need to inform the Tax Credit office.

Where to get help

National Autistic Society – The (NAS) is a great source of information for parents, professionals and those with autism. Alongside their website, they also have a helpline number. The NAS also run workshops for parents and professionals in local areas, such as managing anger. After their child receives a diagnosis if the scheme is run in their area, parents are invited to an information session of the relevant Earlybird course. For children under the age of five years and have yet to start full-time school their parents attend an Earlybird programme. For parents of those aged four until eight their programme is Earlybird Plus and there is another course for parents of those approaching their teenage years. These courses offer an insight into what it is to have autism, developing strategies and parental empowerment. Courses can run for three months and places are limited and may not be available in all areas, the teenage years course is self-referral through your local NAS, however you will be invited for the Earlybird and Earlybird Plus courses in appropriate.

The Local Offer – The Local Offer is an enterprise that seeks to improve SEND services for those ages nought to twenty-five, covering all one hundred and fifty-two authorities in England. Your school or local authority should have details of what this means for your child.

Dentists - A visit to the dentist is scary for most of us, but for children on the spectrum it can be terrifying, especially if they have hypersensitivity. If your child currently visits a regular dentist and isn't coping very well, then you can ask your dentist to refer them to the Specialist Dental Service.

   My children hated the dentist, my son wouldn't let them near him and my daughter from the age of six months onwards would sit on my lap cuddled into my shoulder, screaming. It was actually the dentist that said she wanted to make a referral as she couldn't do anything with them. From the first visit to the specialist dentist the difference was incredible. As in any area of life, it was so easy when we were dealing with someone who knew all about autism and knew how to help. Within two minutes, my daughter was smiling on the dentist chair with a pair of princess sunglasses on. I was so amazed, I actually took a photo. The difference was the calmness of the staff and the long appointment times. At their old dentist, there was never any time to sit and talk them through what was going to happen, after all time is money. The specialist dentist devoted a whole hour to both of them and the room was specifically decorated to be inviting to children, making them relaxed. Unfortunately, my son needed a filling this year, but it wasn't a big deal to him. They talked him through what they were going to do and why and then let him see all the tools and demonstrated what each one did. While the dentist worked, she would count to five and then stop, so that my son wasn't overwhelmed, and she worked at his pace. He could put up his hand at any time to stop, which also helped him feel in control. It has been amazing to witness the progress both children have made.

Independent Parental Special Education Advice – (IPSEA) is an English charity that offers information and support for children and parent/carers of children on the spectrum, especially regarding the laws surrounding special educational needs. Their website offers information and booking for appointments.

Parent Carers Groups – A simple online search, especially on social media can provide you with details of local parent and carer forums that can offer support. It can be useful to be in contact with parents who are going through the same as you and can also feel empowering when you are able to use your experience to help another family through a situation you have already dealt with.

Some Helpful Books – There are lots of helpful books, but I wanted to share the handful that have had a profound effect on myself or my children.

- When My Worries Get Too Big! by Kari Dunn Buron.
- Curious Incident of the dog in the night-time by Mark Haddon.
- Fingers in the Sparkle Jar by Chris Packham.
- Aspergirls by Rudy Simone.
- All Cats have Asperger Syndrome by Kathy Hoopmann.
- Dude I'm an Aspie by Matt Friedman.
- Starving the Anxiety Gremlin by Kate Collins-Donnelly.
- Blame My Brain by Nicola Morgan.

A note from the author

I hope this book will have been of some use to you and that it may continue to be of use as issues arise in the future. One of the benefits of the social world we live in is that there are lots of groups of parent and carers out there who are going through the same as you. Don't be afraid to reach out, you are not alone.

About the author

I live in the South West of England with my husband and two children Asperger's Syndrome. I have written two other novels about autism which are available from Amazon.

- Looking at stars at three in the morning
- I'm dreaming of a Wight Christmas

I have also started up my own company called Stars Autism Services, promoting empowerment, understanding and education amongst parent/carers.

Please feel free to contact me at Stars Autism Services on Facebook, or by email starsautismservices@gmail.com.

Printed in Great Britain
by Amazon